THE HAITI EXPERIMENT

HUGH LOCKE

Amid the
wreckage of a
country once rich
beyond measure,
**a chance to
rebuild.**

HAWKEYE PUBLISHERS

New York

2012

Book website: www.TheHaitiExperiment.com

Facebook page: www.facebook.com/TheHaitiExperiment

ISBN-10: 0988216302
ISBN-13: 978-0-9882163-0-3

Hawkeye Publishers
New York, New York

Published September, 2012

Cover design and illustration by A. F. Cortés.
Back cover photo by William Charles Moss.

To forester, author and environmentalist
Richard St. Barbe Baker (1889–1982),
with warmest thanks for being my mentor in service
to humanity and my guide to a life well lived.

And to Wangari Maathai (1940–2011), founder
of the Green Belt Movement and winner of the
2004 Nobel Peace Prize, with deep gratitude for
your example, your message, and your friendship.

Contents

Prologue

HAITI, 2005. Bright morning sunlight glinted harshly off the rolls of barbed wire topping the barricades on either side of the road as we entered the notorious slum of Cité Soleil, deep in the heart of Haiti's capital city of Port-au-Prince.

Suspicious, youthful eyes peered at us above bandana masks, the wearers' bravado pumped up by the guns they casually, but deliberately, brandished. They had been instructed to let the four men in our red car enter without shooting at us. Happily, all seemed to have got the message. Inside the car with me were three of my Haitian employees, who went by the names of Riro, Jimmy O, and Beaudy. We were all nervous but quiet as we passed through the barricades and followed a masked man on a motorcycle who was to guide us to our destination.

We were on our way to meet Amaral Duclona, the infamous gang leader, known throughout the country by his first name—the most wanted man in Haiti. His bloody reign of terror had kept the police and UN peacekeepers out of Cité Soleil and rival gangs at bay. I was meeting with him to negotiate terms for allowing Yéle Haiti—the organization I had co-founded earlier that year with musicians Wyclef Jean and Jerry Duplessis—to continue bringing in free rice for the local residents who were suffering for lack of food.

We reached Amaral's compound and were escorted into a court-yard. As we entered, about a dozen teenagers toting machine guns were chatting or leaning against the courtyard walls. One of them informed us that Amaral would come out shortly. With dark clothes, sunglasses and wool caps they were clearly intending to look tough, an image not quite matching their youthful appearance.

My long training in protocol, honed over many years by contact with various royal families and a considerable number of heads of state, suppressed any fear that might reasonably have guided my actions. Without thinking, I immediately went around the courtyard and shook hands with each gang member, being sure to make eye contact in the process. My Yéle colleagues chose not to follow my lead and looked on in stunned silence. An interesting detail: holding a machine gun requires both hands, something I quickly realized when each of the gang members had to set down his gun in order to respond to my gesture. A small but useful addition to my protocol experience.

Amaral emerged and greeted me and my colleagues. He was just under six feet tall, rather pudgy, with very dark, pock-marked skin, short hair, and a neatly trimmed beard. I have to admit that I was intrigued to meet someone who was, by action and reputation, the very incarnation of pure evil, who held sway over so many thousands of people. Physically, he did not look the part, but when he began to speak, he exuded both power and charisma.

The meeting with Amaral had been set up from New York by Wyclef Jean, Yéle's co-founder, and one of the few people at that time with the moral authority to reach out to those on all sides of the conflict that had paralyzed Haiti. I knew that Wyclef had spoken by phone in advance with Amaral, but the latter was clearly surprised when we met. It had been arranged that I would call Wyclef on my cell phone. The connection went through and I handed the phone to Amaral. I only learned later that Wyclef had neglected to tell Amaral in advance that I was white. So his first thought on meeting me was that I could not possibly be representing Wyclef, and might even be part of a plot by the UN to capture him. Thankfully, Wyclef was able to convince him that I was, indeed, his trusted representative. I shudder to think what might have happened if cell phone reception had been bad at that moment.

Having established my credentials, I ended the phone conversation with Wyclef. From that moment on, it was just Amaral and me, with Riro serving as interpreter. Beaudy and Jimmy O stayed in the background and took no part in the negotiations. I acknowledged that Yéle was coming into Amaral's territory to deliver free food and expressed gratitude that he was allowing us safe passage. I expressed the hope that this would continue, and then got to the heart of the matter: negotiating the percentage of food that would be given to Amaral to feed his and other gangs. Until that time, we had no formal arrangement with the gangs for any percentage, but had simply given them a few bags of rice from time to time. However, several incidents had alerted us to the need for an understanding in order to continue the operation. After some back and forth, we finally agreed on 15 percent, and shook hands to seal the bargain. This was within the terms I had previously agreed to with the World Food Programme, which provided the rice. And it was considered by all an acceptable cost to be able to continue distributing food in Cité Soleil, since Yéle was the only organization able to get through the barricades at that point.

I thought things were going well and that it was now time to take up the second part of my mission: to explain our plan to have only women receive the food that Yéle was to distribute. Amaral did not take to this idea well at all. In fact, he shook his fist in the air and began shouting, asking me why I would do something so stupid. Two competing thoughts occurred to me at that moment: first, the man has guns; and second, that he would probably respect me more if I stuck to my principles. So I calmly explained that we felt women were more responsible when it came to making sure their families got the food, whereas men were often inclined to sell it. Having stated my case, I then thought it wise to formulate an exit strategy. To this end, I suggested we had probably reached the point where we could agree to disagree on the role of women in food distribution, particularly as I was not asking him to get involved directly in that activity. He smiled and became cordial again.

We said our goodbyes. I got back in the car with my silent colleagues and we headed out. It was only after we passed through the barricades that I phoned my wife, April. I had not told her in advance that I was going to Cité Soleil that day, for fear she would worry. But now I was able to relay the news that the visit had been successful and that I was alive and all in one piece.

Introduction

USA, 2012. The deluge of media-generated images of Haitian people in recent years seems to have coalesced to form a single impression, rather like a Chuck Close photorealist portrait consisting of thousands of smaller individual faces. We see a Haitian face distorted by fear, rage, and suffering, and, on closer inspection, the thousands of individual faces in the portrait portray similar emotions.

Although I have seen many such images over the course of seven and a half years of humanitarian service in Haiti, they are vastly outnumbered by faces expressing fortitude, determination, and joy. My experience there has yielded a very different portrait of Haiti and its people, one that I am honored to be able to share.

My introduction to the country was through two musicians, Wyclef Jean and Jerry Duplessis, with whom I worked to create a charitable organization called Yéle Haiti.

When I began travelling there in late 2004, it was as if the entire country of close to ten million people, living in an area slightly smaller than Belgium, existed in a parallel universe in which poverty, corruption, violence, and hopelessness were the norm. I could move in and out of this universe as easily as a three-and-a-half-hour flight from New York City. But while in Haiti, the most I could do was to help a few individuals and families beat the odds and improve their living conditions.

During that initial period, I was acutely conscious of a set of statistics that served as a kind of protective mantra. Taken together and repeated in sequence, it went something like this: Haiti is the poorest and most densely populated country in the Western hemisphere. Eighty percent of the population is below the poverty line, while 54 percent live in extreme poverty. Every year, Haiti ranks as one of the worst failed states in the world. It is always near the top of the annual list of the most corrupt countries. It is regularly identified as having the second largest income gap between the very rich and the very poor in the world. Unemployment is running at more than 50 percent. The list goes on.

But this statistical interpretation of Haiti is does not reflect the people I met and worked with, who are diligent, resourceful, happy, even optimistic. How could Haiti have become one of the most damaged societies on earth? Why could they not organize themselves as a nation to correct the situation? And how could billions of dollars in foreign aid pour into the country every year and not result in significant and tangible improvement?

Haiti holds a kind of enchantment that is hard to explain, unless you have experienced it yourself. I found myself drawn to the country by a kind of ephemeral and beckoning presence from somewhere beyond the statistics. I started to focus less on the sorrow and began a quest to gain deeper insight into the soul of the country. I asked questions of people from all walks of life everywhere I went. I also started researching the country's history and customs.

What began for me as humanitarian service with Yéle took on a wider dimension. I came to realize that Haiti is a textbook case for understanding the nature and impact of development assistance as a whole. In many ways, Haiti resembles other developing nations that receive money from richer countries and benefit from the operations of the financial institutions those rich countries fund, such as the United Nations, the World Bank, the International Monetary Fund, and the Inter-American Development Bank. But Haiti is the canary in the mineshaft when it comes to the challenges faced by developing countries, whether it is deforestation, colonial oppression, political instability, corruption, hurricanes, earthquakes, or the dark side of development aid that started flowing from richer nations in the early 1960s. It seems that the impact is often disproportionally felt in this beleaguered nation.

My goal in sharing what I learned about development is not to engage in polemics, but rather to try and understand the process in sufficient depth to be able to suggest ways in which it might be improved, not only for the benefit of Haiti.

The bottom line in development aid is that when a rich country gives money to a poor one, there are always strings attached. There is no such thing as pure altruism when it comes to development assistance. This is not unreasonable, depending upon the nature of the strings. Even when dealing with humanitarian aid in response to natural disasters, there are often conditions, although they tend to be less stringent. The simple fact is that the bulk of development funding is tied to the political, military, and commercial interests of the donor country.

My premise in this book is that the entire mechanism for delivering development aid has evolved over time into a bureaucratic and fragmented system that is no longer effective in meeting the objectives of the donors, let alone the recipients. Development funds are meted out in discrete chunks for specific projects which are not viewed in holistic terms by either donor or recipient. Donor countries often send in their own companies, non-profit organizations, experts, and suppliers to implement projects which are one-off in nature and not part of a comprehensive, multi-year national strategy. Thus, a school is not part of an education strategy; a bridge is not part of a national public works plan; a training program for farmers is not part of a broader agricultural initiative; solar panels are not integrated into the national energy grid, and so on. A given project may have a life of two or three years, almost never beyond the term of office of the government of the donor country. And when the funding stops, the project often collapses, either because it cannot be maintained, or because no one knows how, or has the will, to find the new leadership and funding necessary to sustain it. The recipient country has usually had a minimal role in implementing the project in the first place, and so has not benefited by building the domestic capacity in industry, professional services, management, or government oversight that would allow it to continue the project that has been initiated.

Put more simply, development aid is both sides of a carrot-and-stick approach: the "carrot" is money for projects, in return for specified policies and actions on the part of the recipient government; the "stick" is the threat of withdrawal of that money by the donor country, if those policies and actions are not followed.

What I observed in the development system as it now operates, both internationally and in Haiti, is not only incredibly inefficient, but lacks an impact commensurate with the vast sums of money being spent to improve the lives of poor and disenfranchised people. It is equally inefficient in meeting the range of strategic needs of the donor countries. The world has become too complex and interconnected for the simplistic carrot-and-stick system to work.

I would go even further to say that the current overall levels of development funding from donor countries—were the funds to be used more efficiently and in full partnership with the recipient nations—could be reduced by as much as a third and still have a significantly greater impact than at their previous levels.

Over the past decade or so, there have been many calls for a change in development assistance, including the need for ownership of the development process by recipient nations. Donor governments, including the United States, have been enthusiastic in expressing their support for this concept. But it is nowhere to be seen in action and lives only at conferences, summits, and high-level retreats. In order for it to work, there needs to be an entirely new model for delivering aid. Tweaks to the existing system will not have much effect, because the system itself is based on principles that have long outlived their usefulness. We must progress further than the development equivalent of rearranging the deck chairs on the Titanic. What is needed now is a way to experiment with a new system for delivering aid that learns from the past, both from what works and what does not, and incorporates all the checks and balances needed to protect the interests of both funders and recipients as more equal partners in development.

Haiti is the perfect place for this experiment: a country where the ranking on just about every index of individual, family, community well-being, and government efficiency is about the lowest in the world. For once, this is an advantage. If an experiment in changing the way development aid is delivered can succeed here, it could succeed just about anywhere in the world. And Haiti is a small enough country that the experiment would be manageable, the outputs measurable, and the lessons extractable.

This book weaves together several themes. It begins with a short history of Haiti, because this background is key to putting my own story in context, and to understanding the country's current problems. To this is added, from late 2004 onwards, a narrative of my own direct experience in providing humanitarian assistance in Haiti as events unfolded around me. This includes going into the gang-controlled slum of Cité Soleil to deliver food in 2006; supporting a wide range of education services in various parts of the country; helping with the aftermath of the food riots in Port-au-Prince in 2008; overseeing emergency services to around 80,000 of the victims of the January 2010 earthquake—including employing up to 2,000 people at a time from the tent camps; and helping to support the first responders to the cholera outbreak in late 2010.

Over these seven and a half years, it is the experience of working with small-scale farmers that has had the greatest impact in shaping my views of Haiti and development assistance. These farmers represent a significant and untapped potential for reversing the fortunes of the country. With the support and active engagement of The Timberland Company, I led a team that created a community-managed agroforestry program that now generates one million trees a year and has increased the agricultural output of 2,000 participating farmers by as much as 40 percent.

Even though Haiti went from being mostly self-sufficient in food production in the mid-1980s to importing close to 60 percent of what its people now consume, small-scale or "smallholder" farming is still the main source of income for two-thirds of Haiti's working population. We developed a simple system that combines tree planting with an agricultural service to improve food crops, building on the farmers' own long history of intensive small-plot agriculture. And now, the most disadvantaged people in one of the most disadvantaged countries in the world are defying the odds, as they transform their own lives and that of their communities. The results are not only gratifying, but embody practical lessons for Haiti and the rural poor around the world.

In recounting my own work in the fields of education, agriculture, health, and various aspects of emergency assistance—six years with Yéle Haiti and a year and a half with smallholder farmers—I will also share the insights that have led to my current, and admittedly somewhat radical, proposal regarding the changes needed in the field of development assistance. These recommendations come together in the fifth and final chapter, in which I propose Haiti as the subject of a ten-year experiment for exploring a new methodology for delivering development aid that will be of benefit to the entire world—if it succeeds. And if it does not succeed, Haiti is still worthy of having the opportunity to change a destiny that has been handicapped by monumental forces, both internal and external, from the moment its heroic slave revolt launched a new nation in 1804.

I first visited Haiti two centuries later, in November 2004. Two important statistics about the country were added to my list at that time: there were up to fifteen kidnappings a week and the bodies of three or four of those murdered during the night were frequently on display the next day by the side of the main airport road. I confirmed that my life insurance policy was up to date, that my wife knew where to find my will… and began my odyssey.

1

A SHORT HISTORY OF HAITI:

*How It Went From Being One of the Richest Countries
in the World to One of the Poorest*

AYITI, 1492. In telling my own story, I feel I must begin by sharing what I learned of Haiti's history, because it influenced everything I did and continue to do there. I want to assure the reader that this account is not intended to replace the much more comprehensive and better informed works of writers such as Laurent Dubois, Jean Casimir, Jeremy Popkin, Paul Farmer and others. What I am sharing here is more akin to a humanitarian hitchhiker's guide to the universe of Haiti.

The tale begins in 1492, with the arrival of Christopher Columbus on an island inhabited by the indigenous Taino peoples. These local inhabitants called the place Ayiti (pronounced "eye-ee-tee"). Columbus ignored them, claimed the island for Spain, and gave it the Latin name of Hispaniola. With the subsequent arrival of more Europeans, the Taino people, ill treated and enslaved by the settlers, succumbed to new diseases and soon became extinct.

Before their disappearance, the Taino taught settlers their method for preserving meat and fish by smoking it on a wooden frame mounted several feet above an open fire. The frame was made of green wood so that it would not burn. Their word for this sounded like *barbacoa*, according to one Spanish explorer who could only report the phonetic translation because the Taino had no written language. While the etymology of the word is not definitive, the modern word *barbeque* is thought to have evolved from *barbacoa*.

Pirates, buccaneers, and slaves

When it became clear there was no gold to be mined, Spain's interest in Hispaniola started to wane and the island began to attract a range of pirates and buccaneers who established bases there. Pirates were freelance operators who attacked ships flying any flag and kept all their plunder. Buccaneers, on the other hand, were specialized pirates, who attacked mostly Spanish ships and were usually sanctioned by either France or Britain. The sanctioning country received a percentage of the buccaneers' plunder, making them a sort of self-financed and income-generating private-sector naval attack force. Here again, the origin of the name *buccaneer* is likely to have come from the French term *boucan*, referring to the device which these pirates *(boucaniers)* used to smoke their meat.

Soon the French and British governments decided that controlling some or all of the island would allow them to get rid of the non-buccaneer pirates who were disrupting their shipping in the region. Both countries made attempts to take it over from the Spanish. France won the day and in 1664, seized control of the western portion of the island and signed a treaty with Spain in 1697. Thus, what would eventually be the countries of Haiti and the Dominican Republic, sharing the island of Hispaniola, had, by the end of the 17th century, become colonies of France and Spain, respectively. To confuse matters, the colonies shared the same name: Saint-Domingue was the French version of the Spanish name Santo Domingo. Soon Haiti (Saint-Domingue) became very prosperous, while Santo Domingo remained very poor. Ironically, the roles are reversed today, with Haiti the poorest country in the region and the Dominican Republic the richest.

The Saint-Domingue side of the island originally prospered for three reasons: slave labor, irrigation, and commerce. Slaves brought from Africa by the French as free labor worked the plantations and produced valuable agricultural products. The French built an advanced and efficient system of irrigation to supply the water that made the plantations productive. Meanwhile, Europeans had developed an increased appetite for imported sugar, coffee, cocoa, cotton, and indigo, a natural blue dye.

The colony soon became the richest in the Caribbean and the most profitable of all the French colonies in the world; Saint-Domingue in the 18th century was to France what India was to Britain during the same period. Saint-Domingue was the main port in the Western hemisphere for commercial trade with Europe, and the second largest trading partner with the United States after Britain. Saint-Domingue produced some 40 percent of the sugar and 60 percent of the coffee consumed in Europe at that time. Historian Thomas Bender gives a definitive perspective: "Saint-Domingue in the late eighteenth century was per square mile unquestionably the wealthiest place on earth, a wealth that depended upon slave labor cultivating coffee and sugar."

Three distinct groups of people lived in the colony: white colonists, or *blancs*, who came mostly from France; *gens de couleur*, the mixed-race free blacks, or mulatto offspring of white colonists and their slaves; and *slaves*, who worked the plantations and outnumbered the first two groups by a ratio of ten to one. By the late 1700s, there were approximately 10,000 whites, 40,000 free blacks and mulatto, and 500,000 slaves.

For many years, approximately one-third of all African slaves transported across the Atlantic ended up in Saint-Domingue, more than went to the United States. Their language evolved as a patois of French and West African languages, known as Creole. While technically forced by their masters to become Catholics, the majority of slaves embraced the Vodou religion—often transliterated as "voodoo"—which evolved from several practices and beliefs of West Africa.

Three related revolutions

The second half of the 18th century saw a profound change in the colony. It was a time of sweeping social and political upheaval on both sides of the Atlantic. The revolutions in America (1775–1783), France (1789–1799) and Haiti (1791–1804) overlapped, and were in many ways interconnected. The recent New York Historical Society exhibition, Revolution! The Atlantic World Reborn and its accompanying publication by the same name represent a milestone description of the three revolutions as having collectively defined the modern notions of freedom, equality, and human rights.

The call of the French Revolution for liberty, equality, and brotherhood initially extended to free blacks in France's colonies. But this was soon withdrawn under pressure from white plantation owners. It has long been thought that the message of the French Revolution was the direct catalyst for the formation by slaves in Saint-Domingue of the liberation army that launched the Haitian Revolution. Reality is more nuanced. Although the French Revolution no doubt advanced new concepts of freedom that challenged the very notion of slavery, the Haitian Revolution had more practical roots. The mountainous colony had always been a challenge to govern and police, and political upheavals in France were reflected in deep rifts among the colonial forces in Saint-Domingue itself. The whole colony had become unstable, both politically and in terms of security, and the slave population saw a chance to break free. It was not only an ideological response, but a matter of basic survival.

There were other connections between the revolutions as well. Some 500 freed slaves from Haiti (still Saint-Domingue), served with French troops in the American Revolutionary War. Included in the Haitian contingent was a twelve-year-old drummer—or flag bearer, depending on which legend you follow—named Henry Christophe. Along with many of his comrades, he would later fight in the Haitian Revolution.

While revolutions were the front-line story of the day, another was brewing in the background: Britain, France, Spain, and the United States engaged throughout this period in an ongoing high-stakes chess game in which Saint-Domingue, and later Haiti, was one of many pawns. In ever-changing combinations, the four major powers alternately declared war on one another, made peace, signed secret treaties, fought again in a different combination, imposed trade embargoes against each other, provided weapons to enemies of their enemies, made up, and fought again. Regardless of any temporary alignments, the four powers deeply mistrusted each other and each wanted to control or influence Saint-Dominigue and, following its independence, what became known as Haiti.

The leader of the Haitian Revolution was a freed slave named Toussaint Louverture, commonly believed to be the grandson of the King of Benin. Louverture's father, so the story goes, was a prince, who had been captured and sold into slavery. A military and political genius, Toussaint Louverture variously fought the French, repelled a British invasion, allied himself with the Spanish, joined forces with the French, and allied with—and was advised by—the Americans. Among the latter was Alexander Hamilton, a founding father of the United States and the first Secretary of the Treasury. It was Hamilton, who in 1799 sent notes to Louverture on the elements he felt should be included in a constitution for the colony. In 1801, Louverture's forces invaded, and took control of, the Spanish side of the island. Shortly thereafter, he drew up a new constitution that made him governor of the whole island of Hispaniola. Several ideas set out in Hamilton's notes were incorporated in that 1801 Constitution.

Although focused on fighting various major battles throughout his tenure, Louverture was also successful in using paid labor to restore the plantation system, which had been severely damaged in the early stages of the revolution. In addition, he negotiated trade agreements with both Britain and the United States, guaranteeing him the income needed to maintain his large and well-disciplined army.

In 1801, Napoleon Bonaparte sent 50,000 French troops, led by his brother-in-law Charles Leclerc, in a last ditch effort to regain Saint-Domingue. This was the largest single contingent of soldiers ever to have crossed the Atlantic up to that point. They managed to capture Louverture in 1802, but the battle continued under Louverture's principal lieutenant Jean-Jacques Dessalines and, in a stunning reversal, Napoleon's army was defeated in 1803 by an army of freed slaves.

In a world powered by slaves, the Haitian Revolution was a truly seismic event. The largest slave revolt in history had been successful in establishing the world's first black republic. The American and French Revolutions had both accepted slavery, while the Haitian Revolution proclaimed by its actions that all persons are equal and can be the property of no other. This basic human right gave further impetus to the collective forces and ideals of the three revolutions that together went on to change the world.

Birth of a nation

What had been the colony of Saint-Domingue became the modern nation of Haiti on January 1st, 1804. The founding fathers chose the title to honor the island's original Taino inhabitants' name for the island, Ayiti. According to legend, and for reasons lost to history, the French had forbidden the slaves of Saint-Domingue from eating soup. Understandably, the first act of freed slaves on New Year's Day 1804 was to joyously and enthusiastically do just that. To this day, Haitians everywhere still commemorate Independence Day on January 1st by eating a mildly spicy "soup joumou" made from pumpkin or squash.

The Haitian Revolution may have rid the country of slavery, but the full flowering of the revolution was shut down in the first years of independence and has never recovered. For more than 200 years, Haiti has been handicapped by two important factors, one internal and social, the other external and political. These two burdens have undermined the Haitian Revolution from the moment the country achieved independence in 1804 to the present day.

Internally, the country has always been deeply divided between a minority mixed-race elite and a majority poor black population, with almost no middle class. That was the case in 1804 and has changed little to the present day.

From an external perspective, Haiti may be a small country, but its real and perceived strategic importance is disproportionately large. Consequently, it has been used and misused by powerful nations. Starting out as the most valuable French colony, it soon became the global poster child for the dangers of slave rebellion. Early 20th century, Haiti would become a political and military asset as the United States sought to exert influence in the Caribbean. Haiti was used as collateral when the United States and other nations began to wield development assistance as a political weapon during the Cold War—lining up developing countries to be either pro or anti-communist. Today, Haiti is once again key in the struggle between two polarized ideological camps, socialist and capitalist, battling for the political soul of Latin America and the Caribbean.

Freedom from slavery may have been won in 1804, but it was not "paid for" until 1947. Following the revolution, the French government waited until 1825 to formally recognize Haiti as an independent nation and demanded reparations for loss of property, including slaves, in exchange for leaving Haiti alone and for not orchestrating a trade embargo involving France, the U.S. and Britain. Throughout history, slaves have been forced to pay their masters for their own freedom, but it is unprecedented for this arrangement to exist between two nations. Haiti paid France 90 million francs—the current equivalent of approximately US$17 billion—over a period of thirty years from 1853 to 1883, but the repayment of the loans taken out by the government in order to meet its obligations to France continued until 1947. Generations of Haitians bought themselves back from France.

The United States was a major beneficiary of Haiti's battle with the French. In 1803, while in the final stages of what had clearly become a losing cause, Napoleon decided to abandon all plans to build an empire in the New World and sold off the rights to his biggest landholding in the region, the Louisiana territory. The ensuing transaction between Napoleon and then President Thomas Jefferson doubled the size of the United States. Because Jefferson owned slaves, he proceeded to legalize slavery in the Louisiana territory as soon as it passed to US control. Thus, it was not surprising that Jefferson refused to acknowledge Haiti as a legitimate, independent country, a move that was not rectified until Abraham Lincoln did so in 1863. By that time, Haiti had lost its pre-revolutionary status as America's second largest trading partner and fell to 29th.

Britain also regarded a free Haiti as a threat because its valuable colonies in the Caribbean were based on slave-operated plantations. Britain waited until 1833 to recognize Haiti.

External opposition undermining an independent Haiti was only half the story. The other half was provided by Haitians themselves, as their leaders played heroic and tragic roles in equal measure. After winning the final battle against the French following Louverture's capture, Jean-Jacques Dessalines became Haiti's first head of state in 1804. He began as Governor General, but when he heard that Napoleon had crowned himself Emperor, Dessalines had himself crowned Emperor of Haiti, which at that time still included the whole island of Hispaniola.

In the course of his short reign, Dessalines continued Louverture's work of rebuilding the plantations with paid labor. But he was a harsh taskmaster and conditions on the plantations were little better than they had been under slavery. He ordered the massacre of all French whites who remained in the country, resulting in the death of more than 4,000 men, women and children. Dessalines was assassinated in 1806.

The builder king

Henry Christophe—he preferred the English spelling of his first name—was made president in 1807. But within a year, Haiti was divided in half, largely along racial lines. Christophe became president of the "State" of Haiti in the north, while Alexandre Pétion became president of the "Republic" of Haiti in the south. The government of the north was led mostly by former slaves, while that in the south was led by *gens de couleur* and dominated by the mulatto elite. It was ironic, then, that the north, under Christophe, quickly became an authoritarian regime with conscripted labor to run the plantations, while the south, led by Pétion, embarked on a rather liberal policy of land distribution.

During this period, Christophe undertook two great building projects in the north which stand to this day as a tangible legacy of both the heroic and tragic aftermath of the Haitian Revolution. The Citadelle is a majestic fortress built on a mountaintop and designed to fend off future invasions. The Sans-Souci Palace is an immense structure modeled on those of Europe and fit for a king.

Imagine a country of freed slaves, unsure of just how the rest of the world was going to react. It was clear from the outset that they had no natural allies to turn to for help with defense against the major powers, any one of which might decide to invade. The response was to build a military defense system that included some twenty fortresses and installations throughout the country, the centerpiece of which was the Citadelle. Construction began in 1804 under Christophe's supervision, when he was a lieutenant of Dessalines responsible for the north.

The Citadelle Henry, as it became known, is on a scale beyond comprehension for such a small country. It is larger than any other fortress in North or South America, with walls that are 16 feet thick in places and external ramparts that rise 130 feet. It took an estimated 20,000 freed slaves, conscripted into near slave conditions, sixteen years to complete the structure. Military historians now marvel at its sophistication and point out that its design drew on then contemporary military doctrines for fortifications, but combined them in such a way as to represent an entirely original concept. The vast water and food storage capacity of the fortress was sufficient for the survival of those within the fortress for up to a year under siege. Its extraordinary inventory of weapons and munitions, most of which remain intact to this day, made Citadelle Henry a war machine equal to any fortress of its kind at that time anywhere in the world.

For the new republic, the Citadelle Henry was more than a fortress. It quickly became a symbol of black freedom. As a fortress, it never saw battle, but the symbolism endures. And the cost to the new nation is also part of its legacy. Combined with the rest of the defense system, the expenditure of so much financial and human capital on this structure greatly delayed the development of a public sector which would normally have supported a legal system, education, infrastructure, and commerce.

In 1811, Christophe, who had been president of the northern part of the country, had himself crowned the first King of Haiti, which by that time had reverted to its original borders and no longer included Santo Domingo. A brilliant and visionary man—and by all accounts an organizer extraordinaire—Christophe was also a megalomaniac. Burdened by the building of a massive defense system, struggling to rebuild a war-ravaged economy, and simultaneously engaged in ongoing skirmishes against the southern part of the country, he nonetheless decided to take the time and resources not only to declare himself king—which might have involved only the cost of a splendid ceremony—but also to create an entire order of nobility, complete with princes, dukes, and barons. And they all had to have names, and, not having an aristocratic lineage to draw upon, names were invented, such as the Duke of Marmalade and the Count of Limonade. A suitable royal coat of arms and impressive medals and regalia were also required. But it was the royal building plan that strained the new nation to its limits and further prevented the Haitian Revolution from becoming the springboard for the emergence of a nation worthy of the sacrifices made by its liberating army.

Henry I, King of Haiti, was the quintessential royal builder. High on his list of priorities was the construction of a palace—not only one, but several secondary palaces, eight in total, not all of which were completed during his lifetime. And while palaces were essential, he needed to move about the country. Since a king cannot stay just anywhere, he transformed a number of large colonial houses into royal residences. And the nobles—numbering 134 by the end of his reign—also needed proper accommodations that required the renovation and construction of many more fine structures.

Sans-Souci, King Henry's main palace, was located a few miles from where the Citadelle was being built. That a nation of freed slaves could construct a palace equaling the grandeur of those of Europe may be seen as heroic. But it is also the tragic folly of a megalomaniac at the expense of his own people. Viewing only the magnificent building and not the folly, San-Souci or "carefree" in French, is an architectural masterpiece, set amidst terraced formal gardens with vast lawns graced by statuary and fountains. The whole complex included a royal mint, a state council chamber, a chapel, library, dairy, stables, and even the king's private swimming pool. The royal tableau was set against a backdrop of mountains, covered in lush, tropical vegetation laced with clouds of mist.

In 1820, King Henry suffered a stroke that left him partially paralyzed. In his diminished state he began to lose control of his army and within months committed suicide, rather than face an inevitable coup. Legend has it that the king used a silver bullet to take his own life, believing that, as a royal personage, he would not succumb to a regular-issue shell. His palaces were looted by a joyful population and San-Souci was later partly destroyed by an earthquake in 1842. Today, it stands as a hauntingly majestic ruin.

Broken, broke, and occupied

Pétion, the leader of the south, had died in 1818 and was replaced by a mulatto named Jean-Pierre Boyer. Less than a month after King Henry's death, Boyer's troops claimed the north without bloodshed, and Haiti was once again a single nation. Soon after that, Boyer invaded neighboring Santo Domingo, freed its slaves, placing Hispaniola again under one government—until a revolt in Santo Domingo in 1844, which led to the establishment of the modern Dominican Republic.

Boyer actively recruited freed slaves from the United States to settle in Haiti. Nearly 6,000 immigrated, although many returned to the United States after encountering extreme poverty and no assistance from the Haitian government to help them get established.

Following Boyer, the now reunited Haiti had a succession of leaders: presidents, several of whom were dictators, and one self-declared emperor, who commissioned jewelers in France to make a magnificent crown in gold and precious stones. The various leaders did little to change the country's situation, and with little to work with, the odds were stacked against them. The plantations which had been the basis of the colonial economy were never effectively transformed into productive freehold farms. For the first sixty years or so, trade was restricted because the great powers did not want to reward a slave rebellion and risk sending a message to their own slave populations. By the time slavery was winding down and trade restrictions eased, Haiti had been permanently incapacitated.

However, as mentioned earlier, the greatest single economic constraint to Haiti's future development was the debilitating legacy of its US$17 billion payment to France following independence. Payments had to be made in installments over thirty years, at times representing a crippling 80 percent of the national budget. The combination of reduced income, restricted trade, and enormous debt load forced Haiti to take out additional loans from US and European banks in order to cover its operating budget.

But Haiti's problems were by no means all inflicted from abroad. The great divide between the black population and the mulatto elite became more deeply entrenched and codified during this time, with the elite taking near total control of privately held land and the business ventures that had begun to develop as the economy diversified. Successive governments actively participated in preserving this arrangement, out of which grew a culture of pervasive and endemic corruption which flourishes to the present day.

Despite these restraints, the economy improved in the late 1800s and helped to generate three decades of relative stability. During this period there was a flowering of the arts and culture, while democratic institutions and the rule of law gradually emerged. But unrelentingly miserable conditions for the masses gave rise to regional warlords and rural militias known as *cacos*. By 1908, they were making increasingly bold raids into populated areas, often encouraged and funded by one or another of the elite families seeking to protect their own interests. By 1911, the *cacos* had become armies and the country was thrown into revolution. One after another, six presidents in rapid succession were assassinated, blown up, dismembered, or forced to flee the country. Haiti was in turmoil.

In 1915, the United States sent its Marines to occupy Haiti, and stayed on to control the country for another nineteen years. There were a number of reasons for this action: US banks were owed enormous sums by the government of Haiti; various US commercial interests were at risk; a small number of German nationals had become enmeshed in Haiti's commerce and ports and were supposedly in dialogue with the German government as that country sought naval outposts in the region; lastly, the United States was expanding its political influence in Latin America and the Carribbean and had opened the Panama Canal in 1914. The occupation of Haiti did little to help the population in crisis, and their predicament served only as a pretext for the

United States to take over the country to protect its own commercial and political interests.

Whatever the original motive, there were significant benefits to the country from the occupation: US Marines ran the country with admirable efficiency; roads and bridges were constructed; schools and hospitals were built; ports were modernized; and drinking water was brought to urban areas. The downside was that this efficiency extended to the conscription of underpaid labor for construction, the imposition of a new constitution that allowed white and foreign ownership of land, and actions to ensure that an average of 40 percent of state income was allocated for the repayment of loans to US and other foreign banks. Forests covered 60 percent of the country at the start of the occupation, but by its close in 1934, the wholesale cutting of trees for timber export during this period resulted in a reduction of the tree cover to some 30 percent.

The US occupation led to a fascination with Haiti on the part of the American public, as evidenced by contemporary media coverage, particularly such print publications as *National Geographic*. At the same time, Hollywood was greatly expanding its output of movies, particularly with the onset of talkies, and Haitian Vodou proved irresistible. With considerable artistic license, writers invented their own "voodoo" character, patching together snippets of mythology with an invented back story, complete with a zombie "handbook" of what the character could do and not do. Some were blind, others sensitive to light, walked slowly with exaggerated arm movements, could be subdued by salt, Christian crosses, water, sunlight, etc. The result is the zombie as we know it today, and the indispensible zombie sorcerer who has the magic potion that revives the dead and makes them into his slaves, characters that live on in American literature and film, but are not tangible enough in Haiti to warrant royalty payments or a licensing deal. Such characters first appeared in the 1929 novel *The Magic Island* by William Seabrook. The first full-length movie, *White Zombie*, was released in 1932, produced and directed by the brothers Victor and Edward Halperin, with Béla

Lugosi as the zombie master. The whole zombie franchise was revived by George Romero in his 1968 classic *The Night of the Living Dead* and further popularized by Michael Jackson in his seminal 1983 music video for the song "*Thriller*."

Sticking pins in Vodou dolls is another Hollywood invention. Such dolls are sometimes found in the rural folklore or witchcraft traditions of various countries, but have never been a part of Haitian Vodou. Although the image is iconic in popular culture, in reality, the only place one can find Vodou dolls in Haiti is in tourist market stalls.

While the *cacos* rebels waged an ongoing and vigorous guerilla war against the US Marines from their bases in the mountains, it was the onset of the Great Depression that finally ended the occupation. The US economy could not sustain the cost of occupying Haiti. Over several years, the Marines were gradually withdrawn and all had left the country by 1934.

Just as the French had left their mark on the country, so the United States left its own unique legacy. The US Marines can now be credited with being the architects of the dual government model in Haiti whereby a national government is technically in place to run the country, but a completely separate parallel government has the real power, money, and means to make things happen. That the US made improvements is beyond question. But the one thing they did not improve was the capacity of Haitians to continue these improvements after they left: building schools does not begin to fix a completely dysfunctional educational system; establishing hospitals and even a limited health system is commendable, but has no lasting impact if it is run by foreigners; constructing roads is admirable, but of limited value if no local people are trained to maintain them and rebuild sections that are damaged by frequent tropical storms. The U.S. even instituted democratic institutions and a relatively democratic national election was held in 1930, but the resulting government still had no real power.

The Haitian dual government model introduced by the United States has an eerie resonance with the current role of foreign donor governments, international financial institutions, the United Nations, and non-governmental organizations (NGOs) which, together, now serve as the parallel government and act independently of the elected government in Haiti. History has a way of repeating itself.

Falling tyrants and trees

When the American occupying forces left Haiti in 1934, the national government it left behind was a fragile house of cards, with almost no experience at governing, a depleted treasury, a faltering economy, and a large underserved population demanding change. The good and decent men and women who saw public service as a calling were outnumbered and outwitted by the majority of the ruling class, whose expertise in coercion, bribery, scheming, and betrayal kept them in power and in full control of what little was left.

Government from 1934 to 1957 had a revolving door presidency. In and out they went, some lasting only months. Some were ousted in coups, some by excessive greed, and others by secret dealings with Rafael Trujillo, the authoritarian dictator of the Dominican Republic who had an obsessive need to meddle in Haitian affairs during the thirty-one years he held power. The one constant was that each president was defined in large measure by his relationship, good or bad, with the Garde, the national military that had been created and trained by the American occupiers. Their creation marked the first time in Haiti that there had been an armed force that was national and not regional. The rank and file were mostly black and the officers mulatto. For a short time following 1934, the Garde was neutral, but in short order they became a political force which, at some points during this period, seized power and functioned as a military junta, and at others were aligned with one or another candidate for president and ensured their choice was elected.

Clarity of vision often comes in hindsight. It is now obvious that a well trained military, when introduced into a country led by a government kept weak by design, is almost inevitably going to become politicized when there are no checks and balances to keep it neutral. The role of the Garde during this period—renamed the Haitian Army in 1947—should be studied carefully by anyone following the current moves by President Michel Martelly to restore the army.

Another phenomenon from this period that warrants study is the influx of relief funds following Hurricane Hazel in 1954. While these funds principally took the form of loans from foreign commercial banks—and like today's foreign post-disaster grants, these were coupled with loans from the World Bank, the Inter-American Bank and other financial institutions—it is worth noting the effect following the 1954 disaster. The injection of money into a weak and corrupt system led to a feeding frenzy among the elite, with relatively little filtering down to finance infrastructure and human services.

The 1954 hurricane also marks the beginning of the end of Haiti's tree cover, which had once been lush and tropical. The triple forces of poverty, overpopulation, and poor government had resulted in the relentless cutting of trees by earlier generations and this process had gathered momentum during the nineteen-year American occupation ending in 1934. The poor could get cash by cutting down trees and selling them as fuel, particularly charcoal. By the 1950s, the sharply increasing population bought charcoal for cooking because it was cheap. The government failed to build a functioning national power grid, with the result that what little electricity was available was the most expensive in the Caribbean region. The poor could certainly not afford electricity, much less electric stoves and other appliances. The government also failed to provide any support or training for rural farmers, with the result that their yields and income remained low and their poor farming practices contributed to extensive soil erosion. This, in turn, led to the cutting of yet more trees to create arable land. Into this vicious cycle of self-reinforcing pressures on Haiti's forests came the hurricane in 1954. The huge number of felled trees was a boost for the charcoal market at a time of rapid population growth. After the trees toppled by the hurricane had been used up, the charcoal market only increased, and the decimation of trees for fuel and charcoal became even more serious throughout the country. Today, Haiti is one of the only countries in the world that continues to depend on trees for 75 percent of the nation's total energy consumption.

The two Docs

In 1957, the country elected the somewhat unassuming François Duvalier as president. A medical doctor and former Minister of Health, he came from the black majority and was not known for any particularly strong ideology. Behind the scenes, however, he had already begun to show his true nature prior to his election by skillfully securing the support of the military to ensure the outcome. Once in power, he quickly established a domestic reputation as a brutal dictator. "Papa Doc" went on to gain international notoriety as one of the worst tyrants of the modern era. The legacy of his repressive regime, which was followed in lockstep by his son, continues as a taint on the country to the present day. There are too many victims of torture and abuse still alive, and too many families still around to tell the story of those executed without cause, for this tragic period in Haiti's past to be relegated to history.

Duvalier holds a morbid fascination as a unique creation within the global pantheon of dictators. He drew on local Vodou mythology to create a personality cult among the black population, leading people to think he was a *houngan*, or priest, with special powers. He wore dark glasses and an oversize black hat that Haitians associated with Vodou iconography. His personal militia also wore dark glasses and were commonly referred to as the *Tontons Macoute*, after a mythological bogeyman who kidnaps and punishes unruly children. Together, they inflicted a reign of terror on and killed any opponents deemed a threat, from a poor laborer overheard gossiping about his well connected boss, to a teacher who was using a book deemed too progressive. The true number will never be known, but it is estimated that the *Tontons Macoute* murdered at least 30,000 people for Duvalier. Not one of the perpetrators was ever arrested, charged, or put on trial.

With the exception of a few brief periods, the United States backed the Duvalier government from 1957 to 1986 and, because Haiti was deemed important in the fight to contain the spread of communism, it provided an average of US$15 million a year in aid. It is generally thought that more than 90 percent of that money ended up in the personal Swiss bank accounts of Duvalier and his cronies, along with other large amounts that the government took out as loans from foreign banks, ostensibly to help run the country, but which, in reality, ended up in the same accounts.

Duvalier targeted the mulatto elite, winning points with the black majority. But he had no qualms about confiscating the land of poor farmers and giving it to members of the *Tontons Macoute*. No one escaped his totalitarian grip on the country, leading to the first great wave of Haitian emigration to the United States and Canada. This included many educated professionals who might otherwise have been able to help build a middle class.

Duvalier died in 1971 and was succeeded as president by his nineteen-year-old son Jean-Claude, who quickly became known as "Baby Doc." Haiti's own version of Mussolini was now replaced by Mussolini lite. Baby Doc made few changes and delegated most of the day-to-day affairs of state to advisors who had served his father. Terror and murder continued unabated. Corruption was endemic and the mass exodus unceasing. The US government continued its role as the cash machine, interrupted for brief periods when it became too embarrassing. The most notable difference between father and son was the lavish personal lifestyle of Jean-Claude, first as playboy and then, following his marriage to the glamorous Michèle Bennett, as the husband of a high-spending wife, known for her devotion to the financial well-being of the great fashion houses of Europe.

Papa Doc's reign of terror had been largely open for all to see. But that had already begun to change in his later years, so that by the time Baby Doc inherited the mantle of power, the country had a surface patina of stability that masked the darker side of dictatorship. This coincided with an era of tremendous expansion in the tourism industry for both economy-minded vacationers, and those for whom the new term "jet set" had been coined. Haiti was put on the map for the budget crowd with the opening of Club Med in 1975. For the affluent jet setters, there was Habitation Leclerc, a hotel that opened in 1974. Instead of having rooms, it had forty-four separate villas clustered around nineteen swimming pools. It quickly established a reputation as one of the best luxury resorts in the world, with a notorious night-club on the grounds and a high-stakes casino with a black-tie dress code nearby. Possibly the most outrageously extravagant hotel was the Relais de l'Empereur, which featured gold-plated faucets in every room and always had champagne on the breakfast menu. Slim Aarons, a photographer known for chronicling the lifestyles of celebrities of the era, captured the spirit of these oases of hedonistic opulence in numerous photos. Visitors of the time included Elizabeth Taylor, Richard Burton, Mick Jagger, Lillian Hellman, Marlon Brando, and even Bill and Hillary Clinton, who honeymooned there in 1975.

Pontiff, pigs and problems

One visitor who caused a considerable stir during this period was Pope John Paul II. He came in 1983 and famously declared in Creole that "things must change." He went on to give a litany of the country's ills, as a stunned Baby Doc stood helplessly on the sidelines; here was the one person he could not silence or intimidate. Many people still credit the pontiff for emboldening both laymen and clergy to mobilize against the dictatorship.

A broadly based resistance to the Duvalier dictatorship was, indeed, growing, both in Haiti and among the Haitian diaspora living in the U.S., Canada, and Europe. Those in the diaspora were beginning to exert their own political force, particularly in the United States, where they were creating their own media operation as a voice for the Duvalier opposition. Radio broadcasts that could be picked up in Haiti were particularly influential in keeping the resistance movement there informed and united.

Many people point to the slaughter of the country's pig stock as helping to fuel the popular revolt that toppled Baby Doc Duvalier. Known as Creole pigs, or "cochon-planches," these small, black, resilient hogs had long been more than just farm animals, but represented a savings bank that could be sold to pay for school fees, medical emergencies, weddings, or seed for crops. As such, they were a key component of the rural economy. In 1978, a highly contagious swine fever spread from Spain to Cuba to the Dominican Republic, and from there to Haiti, infecting a third of the pigs there. Fearing its spread to the United States, the American government pressed for the killing of all 1.2 million Creole pigs and by 1984 they were all gone. Although a good portion ended up in Duvalier's pocket, the U.S. paid compensation to farmers and introduced new American breeds of pigs unsuited to conditions in Haiti. These new pigs were high maintenance; they would not eat scraps and needed special feed, required frequent trips to the vet, and had to have custom-built shelters. The new pigs died off quickly, the farm economy suffered a tremendous blow, and the Duvalier government was seen as responsible for the disaster.

Around this time, the human immune deficiency virus was identified and AIDS quickly became a global problem. Initial reports pointed the finger at Haiti as the source of the outbreak. Although this was later proved false, the AIDS stigma became a permanent and irreversible facet of Haiti's international image, one that no amount of evidence to the contrary by experts has ever been able to reverse.

Another dimension of Haiti's image took shape during this period, namely, as a country of choice for illegal drug smuggling from South America and other parts of the Caribbean to the United States. Haiti was attractive in this regard, because of its well known economic and political instability, a judicial system that had a standardized rate sheet for corruption, and law enforcement that was not only non-functional, but which included in its ranks high-ranking individuals who were always willing to moonlight. Drug traffickers could feel safe from arrest and prosecution. Today, Haiti is ranked among the four most important countries for illicit drugs entering the United States.

The thirty-year dynastic dictatorship of the Duvaliers finally ended in 1986, when growing opposition to their corrupt regime led to large demonstrations throughout the country. But it was the crumbling structure of the dictatorship itself that concerned the US administration. Their interest was in stability in the Caribbean region, and if that meant shoring up a dictatorship, then that was the order of the day. But if you are going to support a dictatorship, you at least want one that works. Baby Doc was no match for his father. He had lost control and was no longer a good investment on the part of the U.S., which ultimately pressured him to resign and provided a military aircraft to take him and his family to exile in France.

For the next three years a provisional military government ruled Haiti. During this time, the US Central Intelligence Agency set up, trained and financed the Haitian National Intelligence Service— SIN is the French acronym—staffed with officers from the Haitian army and intended to target drug trafficking and political violence. An election scheduled for 1987 was cancelled when SIN-led troops, who had quickly gone astray from their original CIA-inspired mission, massacred an estimated 300 people who had lined up at the polls. The following year a new election was boycotted by all the previous candidates and most of the population. The winner was ousted by the military after only three months. Chaos continued for another two years, assisted in large measure by the SIN troops, who had become major drug traffickers themselves. The ensuing political violence ended with the murder of an estimated 5,000 opponents of the government and those involved in various pro-democracy movements.

The mid 1980s were also important in marking the last point when Haiti grew most of its own food and imported only a small fraction of what it consumed. On his way out the door, Baby Doc dipped his hand into the treasury one last time, forcing the new government to approach the International Monetary Fund (IMF) for a loan. The IMF agreed, but only on condition that Haiti lower its tariffs on imported goods, including food. The single most important crop in Haiti at that time was rice, which was mostly grown by small-scale farmers. With the tariffs lowered, the country was flooded with subsidized rice from the U.S., and in the course of just a few years, thousands of small farmers throughout the country were ruined or reduced to extreme poverty.

Looking back it is clear that, while intended to provide local consumers in developing countries like Haiti with cheaper food sources, the policies of the IMF and other institutions such as the World Bank, by insisting on reduced tariffs on imported goods, had the net result of destroying much of the local agricultural production and ensuring a dependence on subsidized food imports.

Priest on deck

Haiti's presidential election in December 1990 was considered the first in the country's history to be free of massive fraud, violence, and intimidation. Regardless of its abuses in the past, it was the army that made this election possible, assisted by international observers. Jean-Bertrand Aristide, a Roman Catholic priest who embraced liberation theology and who had been a leading figure in opposing the Duvalier regime, won by a landslide. The poor black population was ecstatic that one of their own was in power, while the mulatto elite and the military were largely unhappy at the prospect of any dismantling of their hold on the country, particularly the economy.

Aristide inherited a country, a government, and an economy that had been beaten down for decades, with the final blows delivered by the Duvaliers and their *Tontons Macoute* enforcers. Despite these odds, and within only months of being elected, he was able to deliver much-needed services, began enforcing tax laws, fought drug trafficking, and began to weed out corrupt civil servants. The flow of immigrants to the United States and Canada declined sharply. But his tenure lasted only eight months, at which point Aristide was deposed by a violent military coup, carried out by both the army and the Haitian National Intelligence Service (SIN). He went into exile for almost three years, first to Venezuela and then to the U.S., during which time a military dictatorship ruled Haiti.

With a military junta in power, the Duvaliers were back in all but name. This new reality, combined with a faltering economy, led to a new phrase entering the lexicon of Americans: the term "boat people" now referred to the tens of thousands of desperate, impoverished Haitians attempting to sail in small boats to Florida. Most were stopped—and many saved—by the US coast guard and returned to Haiti. Added to this problem of illegal immigrants was mounting evidence of atrocities by the junta, which led to pressure from the United States and other governments, as well as the United Nations, for the military to step down. This was reinforced by a UN-led oil and arms embargo. Finally, in late 1994, after the arrival in Haiti of a US-led multinational force of 23,000 soldiers that had been authorized by the UN, Aristide was restored as president. By that time, he had left the priesthood and married.

One of the first things Aristide did on his return was to begin disbanding the army. This included the rural constabulary that had originally been set up during the US occupation to ensure law and order in the mountainous rural areas. By January of 1995, the entire army was gone; however, not all weapons were confiscated from decommissioned soldiers and senior army staff, nor were there any severance payments. In many cases, final wages were not even paid, contributing to mass discontent among the ranks, which, within a few years, would coalesce into armed revolt. In place of the army, the country's first civilian police force was launched and trained by an international police force led by Ray Kelly, previously New York City Police Commissioner, and as of this writing serving in that post again. But from the outset, this new civilian force never received sufficient support to become truly effective. This remains the case to the present day.

Cheap food conundrum

American support for restoring Aristide to the presidency in 1994 came with the condition that Haiti further reduce trade barriers and open its economy to food imports, mainly from the United States. In setting this condition, the American government was only following conventional wisdom that dates back to the inception of modern development aid in the early 1960s. The economists, international bankers, and development experts who then had the ear of politicians in rich countries had a basic strategy that has held sway without much change until very recently. Stripped down to basics, it holds that the answer for all poor countries is to focus on urban industrialization as a way out of poverty. In the process, these countries must sacrifice their small-scale local farmers in favor of cheaper food imports from the rich nations, thereby helping to ensure a lower domestic cost of living. In a process called "trade liberalization," high import taxes are set by the rich countries and low import taxes are mandated for poor countries as the most efficient way to adjust commodity flows, this in order to ensure that the rich countries always have enough money to donate to the poor countries. The developing nations that become wealthier will neatly transition to becoming trading partners with donor countries rather than net aid recipients.

This vision for improving the lot of poor or "developing" countries was based on providing money in the form of grants and loans earmarked for the expansion of urban industrialization as a way to create local jobs and products for export. In addition to building factories and the other components of industry, additional investments focused on building the infrastructure needed to provide electricity, roads, ports, and other services that would support urban industrialization. This formula took shape just as large-scale farming in the rich countries began to generate surpluses needing a market, thus fitting neatly into the picture, since poor countries were in need of cheaper food to feed their populations. These recipient countries had too many inefficient small farms. While it might have been possible to help these small-scale farmers improve their productivity, why duplicate the investment that had already been made in the rich countries? Instead, the rule was to lower import tariffs on imported cheap food from rich countries to ensure that it was still cheap when it reached the poor local populations. In order for this formula to work, the poor countries had to agree to restrict any domestic support for small farms and instead encourage migration to the cities so as to increase the labor pool for industry. Any major agricultural investment would be limited to large-scale farms that would produce exclusively for the export market and be limited to crops that would not represent competition for the supplier countries.

In many ways this is not an unreasonable system. Why shouldn't rich countries be able to protect themselves when helping poor countries escape poverty? One answer is because urban industrialization may work in some places, but not everywhere. Moreover, large-scale farming may work in some places, but not if it means sacrificing rural life and small farmers, which are both fundamental components of a healthy economy and the social fabric that nurtures, and is, in turn, supported by, that economy. In the last analysis, the real answer is because the model has so spectacularly failed in so many places and at such a high cost to donor and recipient countries alike. This is precisely what happened in Haiti.

In 1995, Haiti was, and remains today, a rural economy, with roughly 60 percent of the population directly or indirectly dependent on agriculture. The government was pressured by the United States to reduce programs that supported small-scale farmers. At the same time, from 1995 to 2006, the U.S. and other donors allocated only 7 percent of all grants and loans to Haiti for the support of agriculture—mostly large-scale farms geared to export. By 2007, that number had dropped to 2 percent.

Haiti went from being self sufficient in rice, sugar, poultry, corn, beans, and pork in the mid-1980s to importing 58 percent of all the food it now consumes (42 percent is commercial imports and 6 percent is food aid). In the process, it became the largest importer of food from the U.S. in the Caribbean region. Following the second lowering of tariffs in 1995—as part of their compliance for US military support in 1994—it took just ten years for agriculture to decline 40 percent to represent only one-quarter of the economy. During that same period, an estimated 800,000 small farmers had their incomes drastically reduced; many abandoned farming altogether and moved to Port-au-Prince to find work, with the result that Haiti now spends some 80 percent of its export earnings to pay for imported food.

Rice farmers were the hardest hit. The import tariff, as part of the overall 1995 reductions, was reduced to 3 percent. Follow rice from the fields of such American states as Arkansas and Louisiana to the outdoor markets of Haiti and you will learn a great deal about the overall economic and political challenges facing the country today. What began as a trickle in 1986 became a flood in 1995 as US rice began to take over the local market, significantly undercutting what Haitian farmers could sell their product for. The US farmers were benefitting from savings of scale, favorable government policies, the low cost of fuel and related fertilizers and pesticides, and, most of all, they received significant subsidies provided by US taxpayers.

Haiti now imports 82 percent of the rice it consumes, and more than 95 percent of that rice comes from the United States. Based on statistics issued by the US Department of Agriculture, Haiti is the fifth largest market in the world for US rice. The other four markets ahead of Haiti are Mexico, the Middle East, Central America, and Northeast Asia. If you count the markets only by country and not by region, Haiti ranks fourth in the world. And if you break down the various types of rice grown in the U.S., Haiti and Canada are the two largest markets for US "long-grain milled rice," which is known in Haiti as "Miami rice."

Ghosts, guns and gangs

Jean-Bertrand Aristide completed his term as president in February 1996. The Constitution prevented him from serving a consecutive term and he was replaced by René Préval, whom he had previously appointed as his prime minister. This marked the first peaceful transition from one democratically elected president to the next in Haiti's entire history.

While out of office, Aristide formed a new political party called Fanmi Lavalas. Under that banner, he was elected president again in late 2000. This time around, he was perceived as a direct threat to the United States and was vilified in the US, Canadian, and French media.

The basic policy governing US relations with Haiti has not changed in the last 100 years. Whether it was the nineteen-year invasion, supporting a range of innocuous minor dictators, bankrolling a thirty-year state terrorist operation under the Duvaliers, or sending troops to restore Aristide following the coup that cut short his first term as president, the key guiding principle has always been to ensure stability in Haiti in order to protect American financial and political interests. High on the list during the 1915 to 1934 invasion was ensuring that the Haitian government repaid loans to US banks. Later, the Duvaliers might have been unsavory, but they were also stalwarts in the war against communism in a region that was quickly embracing socialism and lauding Cuba for standing up to the United States. In his first term, Aristide was perceived as a maverick who was worth supporting, because he had at least stabilized the country. But by his second term, he was seen as a socialist psychopath, hell bent on subverting the status quo and breaking the monopoly of the elite class who were the natural allies and local partners for US business interests. This was hardly an epiphany born of moral indignation on the part of the US government, but rather a pragmatic realization that stability now meant getting rid of Aristide, funding his opposition, and painting them as besieged champions of democracy and human rights.

The legacy of Aristide will be forever linked with the emergence of the *chimère* during his second term as president. *Chimère* is a Creole word traditionally used to describe a violent and illusive ghost that is impossible to pin down. But by 2000, the word had been commandeered to describe a new breed of armed gangs that operated with impunity outside the law.

There is no other aspect of Haitian history that is more divisive than Aristide's relationship to the *chimère*. It is as if the entire country, joined by the Haitian diaspora, is split into two distinct camps—each with an interpretation that is non-negotiable. It is almost impossible to discuss the matter of gangs without first declaring on which side you fall, either pro- or anti-Aristide. While it may be naïve or audacious— possibly in equal measure—I would like to offer an explanation that does not borrow rhetoric from either side, but which, in the telling, will probably earn the wrath of both.

Rewind now to the US-led invasion in October, 1994 which restored Aristide to power. As described earlier, on his return, the president disbanded the army which had led the coup against him three years earlier. In the process, he also disbanded the police force and the rural constabulary which, throughout the country's history, had always been under the direct control of the military. However corrupt the army and police may have been, the whole country was now, in a matter of months, without any capacity to ensure basic law and order. Into this mix came the 23,000 mostly US soldiers of the multinational force, which was subsequently replaced, beginning in 1995, by successive UN peacekeeping missions. It must be remembered that, historically, and in the case of Haiti, external military forces are brought in to provide stability at the national level, and do not get involved in maintaining public order. Very specifically, these US troops and their UN replacements did not function as a police force.

The United States had once again taken the lead by assembling an international police force that recruited and trained 5,200 new Haitian police officers. The challenge itself was huge: creating an entirely new police force from scratch to replace a corrupt and discredited military police force. After only four months of training, newly minted officers began to be deployed in early 1996. This was the first time in 192 years that Haiti had a civilian police force. But there were problems from the outset. Once in the field, the police had neither the support nor the ongoing training that were needed. They often went months without pay. Before long there were reports of excessive violence, and popular support was waning.

Aristide now had a major problem. Both national security and the new civilian police force were under foreign control, and the latter was not being created fast enough to ensure public order. Foreign control of both meant that neither could be used to gather intelligence. Aristide's response was to create his own militia operation that would combine enforcement and intelligence functions under his direct control.

In short order, Aristide built a militia composed of ordinary citizens, drawn from his power base among the poor. They were not issued uniforms. They had no official badges or identification, nor was there a formal list anywhere on paper of its members. They received no training. There was no hierarchy of officers or regional leadership; each militia unit was autonomous and answered only to Aristide. Their mission was to be a democratic peoples' army, loyal to the president and committed to helping him continue the work of transforming the country to benefit the majority of the poor and disenfranchised.

These were heady days. Militia units were formed across the country and membership soon outnumbered the civilian police force. The militia gained stature as they were used to introduce social programs, launch new schools, and oversee local infrastructure improvements. Their role was easily accepted among the poor, because these were the sort of activities that had long been carried out by informal community leaders—in the absence of functional local government—in the slums and poor regions of the country.

The militia and the police force, each for different reasons, largely excluded former Haitian army soldiers from participation. And those decommissioned soldiers, who often remained in possession of their weapons, began to form an armed, paramilitary rebel force in opposition to the elected government. Like the militia, they also lacked a hierarchy, and autonomous rebel units began popping up around the country. As these rebels began to attack the militia, the latter, in turn, acquired weapons to fight back.

When Aristide ended his term as president in 1996, there was an eclectic mix of players in Haiti: UN peacekeepers who could not take part in police work; a newly created, untrained civilian police force under foreign leadership and largely ineffective; militia units of citizens loyal to the president and granted immunity by him; paramilitary rebel groups made up of former soldiers determined to bring down the government; and, a large number of private security firms, newly formed to protect the families of the elite. And they all had guns. Lots and lots of guns.

By the time Aristide was elected for a second term as president in 2000, yet another category had been added to this set of players. The United States passed legislation in 1996 that toughened the rules for dealing with non-citizens who were convicted of crimes within America's borders. In what would become a steady flow, the first 254 convicted criminals were deported from the US to Haiti in 1997. Most ended up in the slums of Port-au-Prince, and stories abound regarding their unsavory character.

When Aristide took office in early 2001, and despite his original intentions, most of the militia units he had created during his first term had evolved into heavily armed and deadly gangs that were out of control and answered only to themselves. They had gone for several years without much official support and had increasingly found trafficking in illegal drugs to be a reliable and lucrative source of funding, as had many of the ex-soldiers in the rebel groups. By now the gangs were commonly referred to in Haiti as *chimère*, and this name quickly spread internationally as evidence of Aristide's corruption. The irony was that now Aristide had virtually no control over the majority of the gangs and had launched his own armed offensive in order to try and curtail their powers. This, in turn, led many of them to plot his downfall.

A further irony was that many of the elite families who were complaining loudly about instability were quietly funding various *chimère* and rebel groups, often playing both sides against the other. In this messy chess game, the pawns were often moved in a way that made no sense, until the outcome could be seen to benefit one or another rich family.

It is safe to say that the cast of characters eventually included a wide swath of the population from the richest to the poorest. And while Aristide set things in motion by launching and then losing control of his militia operation, he was by no means the architect of their transformation into the *chimère*. It is also true that this overall situation would not have been possible were it not for the deep racial divide that has plagued Haiti since its inception. The poor, black, uneducated, and disenfranchised still constitute the majority of the population; the educated mulatto elite that control the economy are still in the minority; and the middle class is almost non-existent, as its modest membership is continually depleted through immigration to the U.S. and Canada.

Conditions for the poor in Haiti had not improved much in the decade that began in 1990 with Aristide's first election. The poor had pinned their hopes on him then, and now that he was back again, the initial indication was that things were still not likely to improve. This volatile political atmosphere coincided with increasingly violent encounters between various *chimère*, divided now into pro- and anti-

Aristide gangs. In an odd twist, some of the anti-Aristide gangs actually began to ally with previous enemies from among the various paramilitary rebel groups. Pressure quickly grew on any unaligned community leaders or ex-soldiers to transform themselves into either *chimère* or rebels... or be eliminated.

Skirmishes that had earlier been isolated outbursts—during which the local population would seek shelter—increasingly turned into mass riots involving the whole community. Unrest gripped the entire country in late 2003 and into 2004, and it was clear that more and more gangs were turning against Aristide. There are conflicting stories as to whether it was voluntary or forced, but, having earlier sent members of his own family abroad for safety, Aristide and his wife boarded a US military plane in early 2004 and went into exile in South Africa.

Descent into madness

Haiti had been in turmoil leading up to his departure, but after Aristide left, there was utter chaos. Boniface Alexandre became Acting President, but he was unable to control the situation. Public order completely collapsed. Several prisons were emptied and convicted criminals let loose. The police force all but ceased to function. Gangs took control over large sections of Port-au-Prince, setting up armed barricades topped with barbed wire around key slums. Both gangs and rebels, sometimes aided by rogue elements within the police force, began an intense campaign of kidnapping, murder, rape, and looting. Nighttime in the capital was characterized by blackouts, burning tires, gunfire, and fear. Sales of bulletproof vehicles for the elite, government ministers, and the international community soared, while private security firms flourished.

The United Nations sent in a 6,700 member peacekeeping force, formally known as the UN Stabilization Mission in Haiti—MINUSTAH, by its French acronym—that began operation in June 2004. The UN had been a continual presence for many years, but this represented a new level of engagement. The immediate effect was to reduce the scale of chaos and violence. The long-term effect was the formalization within the development community of Haiti's status as a failed state and its transition to what can only be termed "international receivership." This may seem an overstatement, but it is important to understand the scale of the MINUSTAH mission: as of May, 2012, according to the UN, there are now 10,409 uniformed personnel in Haiti, 7,283 troops and 3,126 police. In addition there are 1,917 international and local civilian staff and personnel, plus an additional 226 UN volunteers. Haiti is now the third largest of the 16 UN peacekeeping operations in the world, eclipsed only by Darfur and the Democratic Republic of Congo. MINUSTAH's annual budget is roughly half that of the government of Haiti.

The logic behind the unofficial receivership status—although this will not be found in any official documents or heard from podiums as official policy—is that Haiti is beyond hope and no amount of aid is going to do anything more than prevent the country from becoming the geopolitical equivalent of a black hole. The most overt manifestation of this assumption, reminiscent of the nineteen-year US occupation that began in 1915, is that real power, funding, and decision making rest with a shadow government made up of foreign donor governments, international institutions, the United Nations, and NGOs (non-governmental organizations) which, together, govern the country, separate and apart from the elected government of Haiti.

This was the Haiti I entered in late 2004.

LENDING A HAND:

*My Experience of Humanitarian Service in
Haiti from 2005 to 2009*

HAITI, 2005. The Haiti I first encountered had elements of what I imagine both sets of my grandparents experienced when they pioneered as farmers in Western Canada in the early 1900s—full of hope, arriving in a frontier territory where newcomers had to fend for themselves in harsh conditions. Any NGO representative could simply get off the plane in Haiti in 2005 and set up shop. No need to consult with anybody. No regulations to conform to. No national strategy to plug into. It was indeed a difficult place to work, but all you needed was funding from your home country and a vision of what you thought was needed. It was recommended that you register with the government, but that was nothing more than a formality and was ignored by most NGOs. Haiti was then, as it is now, the wild west of development.

Hand signals for hope

My own Haitian story actually begins in September 2004 in New York City. I had decided, after more than twenty years working on the administrative and policy side of humanitarian service, that it was time to get involved on the ground in developing countries. I had learned much in the course of working for a range of NGOs and UN agencies, and wanted to be more hands-on in the design and delivery of humanitarian programs. To this end, I set up a consulting company focused on creating customized NGOs for celebrities who wanted to give back.

Choosing to hitch my wagon to celebrities might seem counterintuitive when my stated goal was to work on the ground in developing countries. However, my reason was pragmatic. The twenty-year foundation for what I was about to undertake had involved working with an unusual number and range of celebrities and public figures. I had seen first-hand how they could jump start a development project or breathe new life into a stalled humanitarian initiative. I wanted to harness that power by building NGOs that used these individuals to bring immediate visibility to the cause and greatly enhance its fundraising opportunities.

My first step was to turn to Roberto Ramos, with whom I had worked on UN projects and who I knew to be passionately interested in both communications and social issues. Roberto had founded Latin Vox, an advertising communications agency focused on the Hispanic market. Along with his founding partners in the agency, Susan Jaramillo and Andres Cortés, we formed Orsa Consultants. The word *orsa* is Latin for "new undertakings"—not to be confused with "orca" the killer whale, as some thought.

The ink was not dry on the plans for Orsa Consultants, when I was introduced by a friend to the singer, Wyclef Jean. Knowing little about hip-hop musicians, and never having heard his name, I had to take my friend's word that Wyclef was well known.

I first sat down to talk with him at Platinum Sound Recording Studios in New York, owned by Wyclef's cousin and fellow musician and producer, Jerry Duplessis. We met in a room full of high-tech recording equipment, lights, buttons, and levers, reminiscent of the bridge on Star Trek. I soon learned that Wyclef and Jerry were an inseparable duo. They grew up in the same village in Haiti and came together to America. Both had become successful and wanted now to give back to their native country. Specifically, they wanted to mount a major concert in Haiti that would give hope to the beleaguered population. They asked if I would produce the concert.

Only a month earlier, I had produced a concert at Lincoln Center in New York City featuring indigenous musicians from around the world and before that, a tribute concert to Nelson Mandela at the

United Nations highlighting the work of UNICEF. At the suggestion of a concert in Haiti, I immediately went into event mode and began thinking about how to extend the impact from the general intent of "hope" to more specific support for education and social justice programs. But I caught myself. This was something I had vowed to avoid in my new career phase, namely, producing one-time big events that promised to support good causes, but which have little or no lasting impact. So I explained to Wyclef and Jerry that, in my opinion, the better course of action would be to start by using Wyclef's celebrity status as the catalyst to build an organization that would contribute to improving conditions in Haiti, and then, once established, to use concerts in Haiti and overseas to promote the organization and raise money for it. Two hours later, we had designed the basic structure that became our road map for the next six years.

Wyclef was clearly the front man. He had been part of a hip-hop trio called the Fugees that had risen to fame in the mid-1990s. When the group folded, Wyclef went on to launch a successful solo career. In our meeting he struck me as charismatic and charming, wearing his success comfortably, but without the aloofness that often comes with success. Jerry, who had played backup bass for the Fugees, was equally strong, but clearly in a supporting role—serving as Wyclef's business partner, fellow producer, and muse.

Up to this point I was only dimly aware of hip-hop as something vaguely threatening and foreign to my experience, a small entry in a miscellaneous file in my mind. It involved discordant "rap" music that seemed angry and belligerent, abusive of women, full of expletives and fixated on gaudy, oversized jewelry for men. But once thrown into this new world, I found it much more fascinating and engaging than I had anticipated.

Like any major cultural phenomenon, hip-hop has rules of conduct that define who is considered part of the community, their rank within it, how people should conduct themselves, and how they relate to those outside. With Wyclef and Jerry as my guides, I quickly learned that much of what was in my miscellaneous file was inaccurate. This tall white guy from a privileged background was welcomed into a largely black community and embraced without any reservations that I could discern. Bravado and swearing were employed with considerable theatricality, but direct personal interactions were conducted with an old fashioned politeness that echoed the 1950s.

Many people seemed to have nicknames. Wyclef was "Clef," as in the musical symbol. Jerry was "Jerry Wonder." Wyclef's bodyguard, an intimidating physical presence, but an exceptionally kind and thoughtful person, was "Beast." I was given my own nickname by Wyclef when he began to refer to me as "HughLocke," combining both my names into one word. It felt like a rite of initiation.

I came to appreciate rap as a form of urban poetry that allowed black youth to have their own authentic voice. There were many slang words and abbreviations that were common parlance, but everyone was patient in translating for me. I even learned the complex series of movements that begin with a handshake between two men, ending in a hug. The same ritual does not apply when meeting women, who were usually greeted with a simple hand shake, followed by an optional hug.

That first meeting with Wyclef and Jerry at Platinum Studios impressed on me the unique potential of hip-hop to improve people's lives. And Orsa Consultants—with the help of Roberto, Susan and Andres and their expertise in advertising and communications—would help Wyclef and other celebrities who wanted to improve conditions in their countries of origin to be viewed as a brand. The NGO vehicle created had to have the brand presence to attract wide public support because of the celebrities themselves and, by extension, their capacity to raise funds.

Consequently, our first task was to create the brand for this new Haiti-focused organization. The Wyclef Jean Foundation was already incorporated in the United States as a charity focused on providing music training for underprivileged youth in New York, although it had not been active for several years. I explained to Wyclef that, unless he was a Bill Gates-style philanthropist and wanted to fund the entire enterprise himself, no one would support something bearing his name. We needed a new brand that was an extension of Wyclef and his personality and stage persona, but also capable of delivering services that would assist Haitian people to improve their conditions.

By going through all the songs Wyclef had written, we finally settled on the word "yéle," a word he had made up meaning "a cry for freedom." The song by this name was one of his biggest solo hits, with the added advantage of being well known throughout Haiti. We combined the word with the name of the country, and came up with "Yéle Haiti." One of the great things about an invented word is that no one else is using it and there are no secondary affiliations or meanings to worry about.

Next we had to design a logo that would be hip, street smart, and also be understood by people who are illiterate. There were many sessions with Wyclef and Jerry looking at concept illustrations laid out on the floor at the Platinum Sound studio, but the final version took shape after Wyclef asked that the logo incorporate a hand gesture that could have a life of its own.

The hand with all fingers extended can mean "stop," but, in combination with the heart, we intended it to mean "stop the violence." The heart is also a traditional Vodou symbol instantly recognizable to Haitians. The other hand forms the classic peace sign.

A great logo is nothing without a great organization. The dynamic between the logo and what soon became a great organization created powerful synergy. As Yéle's programs began to be noticed, our logo quickly became one of the best known symbols throughout the entire country. More importantly, it was accepted as a symbol that represented the masses:

one of their own, Wyclef, had come back to help them. When an image starts being used by people who have nothing to do with the organization, you know it has entered the popular culture; our logo began to show up in paintings sold on the street, on greeting cards for sale in markets, in spray-painted graffiti, and even in embroidered on exuberantly designed tablecloths with matching coasters. People, especially youth, used the hand symbol as a greeting, one hand with fingers extended, with the other forming a peace symbol pointing towards the extended hand. Kids would pose for a photo making the sign, and Haitians at Wyclef's performances throughout North America and Europe would make the gesture. It was everywhere. I came to realize that the Yéle logo had taken on additional meaning for many Haitians, one that transcended our organization: it symbolized hope and the possibility of change.

Charting the course

With the name and logo in place, it was time to create programs. To this end, I made my first trip to Haiti in November 2004, with Roberto, but without Wyclef or Jerry, because I wanted to explore the country for myself. I wanted to determine the kinds of programs and organizational structure that would allow Yéle Haiti to make a difference in people's lives.

Before leaving, however, I reached out to my network of development professionals and received three key pieces of advice. First, I would need a bullet proof car and an armed body guard when leaving the airport in Port-au-Prince, as there was an average of fifteen kidnappings a week during that period; second, caution was advised in dealing with Haitian charities, since an estimated 70 to 80 percent of all domestic NGOs at that time were fictitious, created only to siphon money from international donors; finally, a meeting was suggested with John Currelly, then Country Director of one of the very few effective NGOs, the Pan American Development Foundation (PADF).

I have travelled extensively in connection with my work with NGOs, and have seen slums and poverty up close in many parts of the world. But exposure to the extreme poverty in Haiti was a harrowing experience. Although only a speck on the map of the Western Hemisphere, Haiti has the distinction of being the poorest in that region. The kind of poverty you expect in parts of distant Africa or Asia is here on the doorstep of the United States, only an hour's plane ride from Miami or three and a half hours from New York.

Within days, I felt a choking sense of outrage at the terrible conditions faced by the majority of Haitians. As this sense of injustice grew, I felt a shift within myself. I was not just setting out to create an organization that would allow Wyclef and Jerry to serve their country. I was surprised to find myself personally invested in a mission to give the people of Haiti the tools that would give them better odds to escape inexorable poverty, no matter how hard they worked. And so, as the first chapter of Yéle's work in Haiti was about to unfold, I became a full-fledged partner with Wyclef and Jerry, a dynamic that shaped the organization as it evolved.

In 2004, Port-au-Prince had approximately 2.8 million residents with a social fabric reflecting the population of the country as a whole. The vast majority of the city's people live in extreme poverty in slums. Relatively fewer live in middle-class conditions. An even tinier minority, mostly mulatto, or light-skinned, mixed-race Haitians form the monied elite and live in homes that would not be out of place in the wealthier sections of Florida or California. Haiti may be classed as the poorest country in the Western hemisphere, but, according to some economists, it ranks second globally for the widest income gap between rich and poor.

I did take up the recommendation to meet with John Currelly, Country Director of the Pan American Development Foundation (PADF). It was immediately apparent, after discovering our shared Canadian heritage, that John had a wealth of practical experience from his several decades living and working in Haiti. And his passion for the country and its people was equally evident. It seemed as if the forces in the universe were aligning to generate the thunderbolt of inspiration that transforms multiple variables into a coherent plan. Three fundamental concepts that would shape Yéle for the coming years took shape at that meeting. First, we would focus our efforts in one of the areas of greatest need, namely, education. Second, Yéle would be more effective if we partnered with existing NGOs rather than operating unilaterally. Finally, Wyclef's unique standing as a cultural icon in Haiti could be used to raise the profile of our NGO partners as well as key sectors of NGO service, such as education, rather than for promoting Yéle as a stand-alone organization.

Having now determined our general direction, we set about creating the structure for delivering programs and managing the operation. The existing Wyclef Jean Foundation had been registered as a non-profit charitable organization in the United States, but was technically on hold because its modest activities did not justify reporting to the U.S. Internal Revenue Service. We decided to revive the original charity, rename it the Yéle Haiti Foundation, and establish a separate branch in Haiti. I became Executive Director of the new Haitian operation, working with my Orsa team, and happily left the US branch to a team appointed by Wyclef and Jerry.

Mixtape strategy

Yéle Haiti's official launch took place in Port-au-Prince on January 10, 2005. This was my first trip to Haiti with Wyclef, and the first time I witnessed the extraordinary response he received from the local population. Everywhere we went, huge crowds would appear within minutes of an unscheduled appearance. But "crowd" does not begin to describe the thronging masses shouting their adoration for him. They were proud of this Haitian who was born one of them, left the country at an early age, became rich and famous—but who did not forget his origins.

Wyclef and his cousin Jerry both came from Lasserre, a village not far from Port-au-Prince. Their parents had first emigrated to the United States and then sent for the boys. But instead of distancing himself from his homeland and feeling a stigma about his heritage, Wyclef chose a different path, and will be remembered for generations for helping to make Haitians proud to be Haitian. In 1997, the Fugees won a Grammy for their album *The Score*, and Wyclef appeared on stage to accept the award wrapped in a Haitian flag. He was unquestionably the best known non-political Haitian in the world at that time, and he used his global platform to proclaim his heritage. Suddenly, for a generation of young Haitian Americans and Canadians whose parents hardly spoke about their homeland, it was cool to be Haitian.

Although he had not been part of my cultural radar until we met, Wyclef was already an international icon. But as is so often the case, his new status came with people's expectations of a role beyond music. I was with him for six years as he struggled to balance his role as a musician with his own, and other peoples' expectations of him as an advocate for Haiti.

Wyclef and Jerry introduced me to Haiti through their eyes. With each new level of engagement with the country, they would share insights that kept me on the learning fast track. Our relationship was that of three distinct professionals who, while not close personally, worked closely together. It was as if we all understood that if I was to be effective, I had to stay out of the orbit of their immediate circle of friends and advisors, some of whom were clearly in the category of entourage.

One of my early lessons came when we were preparing the launch of Yéle in Haiti. Part of my professional background includes public relations and event production, and I drew on this experience when mapping out the media strategy for the launch. I explained to Wyclef that we would issue a press release on the day of the event for the Haitian media. He laughed and said I could follow that path if I wanted to, but that he had a way to reach the population without going through the media. It was called a mixtape. This, he explained, was an art form with close ties to hip-hop, in which one compiles songs and then records a commentary between the songs, and sometimes over them, to convey a message or theme. The form apparently originates with DJs who typically comment as they present song selections.

Unfamiliar with DJs, and never having heard one perform in a club, it fell to Wyclef to patiently educate me. He explained that he would create a mixtape that would include some of his own songs, as well as those of other artists, and that he would record the spoken commentary himself and use it as a way to explain the goals and programs of Yéle to the population.

Once again, I went on automatic PR pilot and began to plan the production of quantities of CDs of the mixtape to distribute to radio and television stations throughout Haiti. Wyclef laughed and explained that we needed only ten copies that he would have distributed to the major music bootleggers in Port-au-Prince. They, in turn, would sell bootlegged copies as tapes and CDs to the population, including the drivers of the popular tap-tap buses and converted pick-up trucks that the poor used for cheap transport. These privately owned, highly decorated vehicles almost always play music and are known to air the latest hits.

Wyclef created the mixtape using my outline of Yéle's upcoming programs, interpreting it in his uniquely creative style, in Creole, the language of Haiti's poor. Ten copies were distributed to bootleggers and within days we were getting reports that it was selling in all the markets and playing in the tap-taps. Radio stations began picking up this new hit on the streets. Wyclef was a genius at communicating with the poor in a direct, efficient, and authentic way. I was to learn much more from him over the years in this regard.

In my own defense, we still issued a beautifully crafted press release that was a classic of its genre. The document was very helpful for the international media representatives who attended the launch, but who were not likely to be riding tap-taps or dealing with bootleggers in the local markets.

Focus on education

If you want to start somewhere to make a difference in Haiti, education is a good choice.

The overall statistics about Haiti are scary, but when you drill down in education, you begin to get a sense of exactly how grinding and unrelenting poverty affects families. Haiti is one of the only countries left in the world where everyone, including the poorest of the poor, must pay to send their children to school. There are between

18,000 and 22,000 schools in Haiti, although to this day the exact number remains unknown. All require tuition fees. About 85 percent are private and require full tuition, while the remaining state schools charge considerably lower fees, but are still not entirely free.

One of the largest expenditures for the majority of Haitian families is the cost of sending their children to school. On average, low income families spend some 40 percent of their annual income on education. Many of these families are faced with the agonizing choice of which children to educate when they cannot afford to pay for all. At present there are between 2 and 2.5 million children in primary school and an estimated 400,000 children who should be enrolled, but are not. The majority of children not in school are from families where other siblings do attend; but the parents cannot afford tuition for all their offspring.

During the school year there is a scene that is repeated early each morning throughout the entire country. From millions of humble dwellings in rural areas, villages, towns, and cities emerge children, dressed in perfectly clean and pressed school uniforms. The girls frequently have ribbons or other decorations in their hair to match their uniforms, the same elements often added to their white socks. To see them, one would think they came from affluent homes. But these immaculately dressed boys and girls make their way along dusty roads, past open sewers and piles of garbage, and through the relaxed chaos of street markets, all part of a daily ritual that embodies the collective hopes of the poor. Everyone taking in the scene shares the same dream: if only we could educate our children, no matter what the sacrifice, they might escape the poverty that we continue to endure.

The millions of children in this daily ritual arrive at schools that have changed little in the past two hundred years. Most have no electricity, no water supply, and no plumbing. In a system put in place in the early 1800s, the twin pillars of education continue to be memorization and corporal punishment. The majority of teachers are not qualified to teach, with only roughly 40 percent ever having completed grade six. Less than ten percent of teachers in Haiti have ever received any formal teacher training, and memorization is often the most they can manage. Added to this, a whip sits on the desk of almost every teacher in the country. It is in frequent use, because they have never been taught alternatives for managing their pupils.

There are many skilled and dedicated teachers in Haiti, but they are in the minority. The Ministry of Education tries its best, but without funding or expertise, has little impact. Barely half the schools in the country are even registered with the ministry, and many of those that are registered go for decades without a visit from education officials. Standards exist on paper for both curriculum content and school management, but there is little capacity to either monitor or enforce these standards on a national scale.

Given the enormity of the challenge, my goal was to seek out several of the top NGO-implemented education programs in the country and provide them with funding, while using Wyclef's celebrity to bring attention to their work.

Once again, John Currelly helped by suggesting that Gonaïves was the appropriate place to begin. This northern coastal city of around 200,000 people is where Jean-Jacques Dessalines declared the independence of Haiti on January 1, 1804. It had been hard hit by Hurricane Jeanne in September 2004. Surrounded by mountains that form a bowl, the sides of which have been stripped of all trees, three-quarters of Gonaïves was flooded by the severe rains that accompanied the hurricane. A thick layer of mud was left by the receding flood waters. Schools had been particularly hard hit, with many destroyed or damaged. Because the local economy was disrupted, many families were left without the means to pay for their children's education.

Yéle's first major operation was to be a collaboration with three other NGOs to undertake the comprehensive rebuilding of damaged school buildings, to put children in school by paying for their tuition, and to upgrade teachers' skills. Yéle's role would be to raise the funds and have our partner NGOs implement the program—with Wyclef helping to raise the profile of the combined operation and highlight the overall needs in the education field.

Author photo.

The first 3,600 students sponsored by Yéle Haiti for school in Gonaïves in 2005 through Fonds de Parrainage National. Later the program expanded to include almost 7,000 students in five cities (2006 to 2009).

Sebastian Petion.

Yéle partnered with the Bureau de Nutrition et Développement (BND) to deliver food supplied by the World Food Programme to vulnerable families in Port-au-Prince slums (2005 to 2009).

Sebastian Petion.

Rapper Jimmy O using hip-hop to deliver social messages. He and his group toured Haiti performing songs about HIV/AIDS awareness and safe sex (2006 to 2007).

Sebastian Petion.

The hip-hop competition for songs about picking up garbage and protecting the environment—a national sensation in 2006. The final event was televised live and the songs aired on nationwide radio.

Louis Dario Louis.

Wyclef and author Hugh Locke on stage at YéleFest 2006 in Jacmel. He gave me my first lines of Creole, and I apparently told the audience that, "I like rice, beans and kalalou."

Sebastian Petion.

Actor Matt Damon (center) and Wyclef (in cap) helping to unload rice in the city of Cabaret following the massive hurricane damage in Haiti in 2008.

Sebastian Petion.

Yéle collaborated with the Jacmel Film Festival (now the Ciné Institute) to project free outdoor films on social themes, using a mobile projector (2006 to 2008).

Sebastian Petion.

Author Hugh Locke with primary school girls sponsored by Yéle when the program expanded from its origins in Gonaïves to include Port-au-Prince (2006).

In addition, Yéle, in this case, was creating a partnership among three NGOs that had not previously worked together. The Pan American Development Foundation (PADF) already had a grant from the US Government to rebuild ten storm-damaged schools in Gonaïves; Yéle added an equal amount of funding and we set out to rebuild a combined total of twenty schools. Fonds de Parrainage National (FPN), led by educator Antoine Levelt, specialized in providing tuition scholarships, school supplies, tutoring, improved learning conditions and school operation for children in primary school. We agreed to sponsor 3,600 students using their services. Another NGO, Le Centre d'Apprentissage et de Formation Pour la Transformation (CAFT) specialized in on-site teacher training; their director, Linda Gershuny, agreed that we would sponsor their training program in fifteen schools.

Beginning in January 2005, I made regular trips to Gonaïves in the course of setting up the program and then overseeing its implementation. The road from Port-au-Prince had always been bad but, following the 2004 hurricane, for the last few hours of the journey, it could hardly be called a road. It was more like a trail passing through and around craters, navigating abandoned wrecks of trucks and buses, and driving through sections of water that you prayed were not concealing large holes. Meanwhile, the security situation was still unstable and kidnapping was always a possibility. If we came across an old lady crossing the road with a goat, my driver refused to slow down, despite my protests. He explained that it could be a trap, and men with guns might be ready to jump out if we stopped to help. Although we did no harm to old ladies or goats, I always felt pangs of conscience when we routinely sped past everyone, regardless of their apparent need.

Working with the above three NGOs, we knew it would be important to engage the community from the outset and not just spring our program on them, as this could, in and of itself, arouse suspicions as to our motives. So we began to bring regional representatives of the Ministry of Education on board and to place ads in the local newspaper and on radio to announce that any school in Gonaïves could apply for one, or all three, of the program elements—

school rebuilding, student scholarships, and/or teacher training. The ads also included details about how the schools would be chosen. Hundreds of applications were received, and it was a proud moment, indeed, when we held a ceremony at which I handed certificates to the schools that had been chosen.

But the full impact of what we were doing really hit home when I asked Antoine Levelt to arrange a group photo with all 3,600 of the children whose tuition we were sponsoring.

The children came from several schools around Gonaïves, and we assembled them in one large school courtyard. I had asked for a platform to be built to provide a good vantage point for the photo, but when I arrived on the appointed day with my staff and a photographer, the platform was still not completed, even though all 3,600 children had arrived and were standing patiently in orderly rows. The platform consisted of two large sheets of plywood held up by a small forest of twenty-foot high vertical posts hewn from tree trunks and cross braced with rough cut lumber. Stairs made of split logs went up one side of the construction. When the last step was nailed in place, I was invited to be the first to climb up. Even before I got to the top, I could feel the whole structure swaying back and forth, suggesting potential imminent collapse. I estimated the range of movement at the top to be at least a foot and a half. While I was willing to risk my own safety, I certainly could not ask that of the others, so told my colleagues, including the photographer, to stay below. I had my own camera and was determined to take the picture myself.

Seeing a large tree branch hanging close to one side of the platform, I carefully navigated along the moving platform so that it was within reach. If the whole structure fell, I could at least grab it and attempt to avoid injury. With the platform continuing to sway, I found my sea legs and finally managed to relax long enough to take in the panorama before me: the sea of children who, but for our support, would not be in school. This was the real and tangible impact of Yéle. I was overcome with a sense of gratitude to have been a part of making it happen. Tears flowed freely as I stood on the swaying platform, holding my camera still enough to take a picture of those innocent and happy children who represented the hope of Haiti.

After the first year, we could not have foreseen the results of the informal survey of selected parents of the students sponsored through our Gonaïves program. Predictably, the majority were happy about the school renovations, but most indicated that they thought the government should have been doing this work; their gratitude towards Yéle was mixed with resentment towards the government for not doing its job. The scholarships were similarly well received, but also with the caveat that the government should have been doing more to support education in Haiti. But teacher training came in for copious praise. As students began to express more enthusiasm about school, a number of parents had gone to investigate what might have brought about this change in their children's attitude. Parents who visited different schools reported to others that not only were teachers learning new methods of discipline and abandoning the whip, but that they were being encouraged to drop the severe formality of 19th century French teaching methods and were using what could loosely be termed "experiential learning." This approach encourages teacher to make learning more applicable to every day experience by, for example, using stones from the courtyard to demonstrate addition and subtraction. The stones had always been there, but it took the staff from CAFT to give teachers permission to pick them up and use them in the classroom. Parents identified the change in their children as a direct result of the changes brought about by teacher training.

The twenty schools in Gonaïves were rebuilt within a year and a half. We continued the scholarship program for four more years, expanding it to cover almost 7,000 students in five cities, including Gonaïves. We continued the teacher training for two more years and, based on community feedback, expanded it to include schools in Port-au-Prince as well.

The program we began in Gonaïves was only one component of our education strategy. I had come across several other NGOs with very innovative programs that I could see were already having an impact and could do even more if they had additional funding. We adopted four of these NGO programs and provided ongoing financial support to each over a five year period.

Maryse Pénette-Kedar and her father, Max Pénette, had convinced the Ministry of Justice and Public Security to let them take over the management of a boy's prison in Port-au-Prince and turn it into a rehabilitation center. Gangs in the slums of Port-au-Prince were conscripting boys as young as ten, first giving them food in exchange for simple tasks and then getting them hooked on drugs and forcing them to become the equivalent of child soldiers. In early 2005, there were ninety-four such boys from ten to seventeen in four cells originally designed to hold ten inmates each. Conditions were like a scene from *Les Misérables* (the book, not the musical) when Maryse and Max formed the Progress and Development Foundation (PRODEV) to take it over. Yéle helped provide a portion of their funding, allowing them to set up a school and vocational training for the boys, get them medical attention, build new bathroom facilities, and establish modest legal representation. Maryse also served as Yéle's president for the first four years, which was an invaluable contribution.

I remember a conversation at the jail with one twelve-year-old year old boy with a particularly angelic face. His name was Ricardo. I asked him why he was there. He said he did not know. He insisted that he had done nothing wrong. I pressed him by asking if he had ever killed anyone, as I knew that was why he had been incarcerated. Without a moment's hesitation, he said he had killed a few cops; but he remained puzzled as to why that counted against him, because they were the enemy. This was the reasoning of a child who should have been trying to understand why he should not give another child a black eye, but instead needed help to understand that cops are people too.

The walls of the boys' prison collapsed during the January, 2010 earthquake and all escaped. I like to think they were better prepared to start a new life that did not involve crime as their only employment option. In the last few years, PRODEV has created two new model schools as a base from which to help improve the curriculum and teaching standards throughout the country.

Former soccer star Robert (Boby) Duval, the founder of L'Athlétique d'Haiti, is one of my heroes. He comes from the wealthy elite of Haiti, but instead of staying within that protected environment, made a lifelong commitment to help youth from the slums improve their lot in life through sports. He built a soccer facility in an area called Drouillard, adjacent to the slum of Cité Soleil. He helps these extremely poor youngsters by giving them the chance to play soccer and other sports, and the sense of self worth and dignity that comes with it. What Boby has built for the very poor is unequaled in all of Haiti; other than a few elite private schools, only the national soccer team has the equivalent level of service for its players. Yéle provided core funding to this program for five years. Today, the original L'Athlétique d'Haiti, in addition to satellite operations that have been added in other parts of the country, provides sports and leadership programs for around 2,000 youth a day.

Philippe Leon and Serge Cantave were enthusiastic members of a motorcycle club and would ride their bikes on weekends to places like the mountainous Seguin region, home to Haiti's last remaining pine forest. They eventually formed an organization, Fondation Seguin, to help preserve this fragile ecosystem. Yéle provided financial support that allowed them to take groups of students from Port-au-Prince on three-day excursions to the Seguin area where they planted trees and learned about the environment. The pine forests there are very unusual in that they are also home to very large yucca plants. When the yuccas are in bloom, their bright orange flowers resemble pom poms atop stems up to twelve feet high. It left me thinking of Dr. Seuss's book *The Lorax* that I had read in my youth.

Conor Bohan founded the Haitian Education & Leadership Program (HELP), an organization that provides full needs-based university scholarships for the top high school graduates in the country— and not only scholarships. They created a center in Port-au-Prince where these students have access to computers and a safe place to study, neither of which can be taken for granted in Haiti. The students also receive assistance with housing and living expenses, because students from poor families have very limited resources. Yéle sponsored several students each year. There are two particularly admirable aspects of the program: there is a 100 percent employment rate for university graduates and, upon graduating, the students become part of an ongoing alumni program through HELP that encourages volunteering.

Beginning in 2005, Yéle was able to support this full slate of funded educational programs thanks to a generous corporate sponsor, a Haitian cell phone company called Comcel—the name of which was later changed to Voilà. The credit for finding them goes to Gwynne Beatty, who had joined the Orsa team a few months before Yéle's launch. I created a business plan for the organization that mapped out the education programs, operating budget, and the role of Wyclef as founder and spokesperson. Armed with this document, Gwynne set out to cold call every company she could find that had interests in Haiti. With relentless energy and efficiency, she soon found a company that was keenly interested in Yéle.

Comcel/Voilà was a subsidiary of the privately held US company Trilogy International Partners, whose CEO, Brad Horwitz, had previously made his mark in the mobile phone sector in the United States. Now, his focus was mobile service in developing countries, with Haiti just one of several places in which he operated. Happily for us, Brad was that rare combination of an extremely successful business person with a strong social conscience. The core funding for Yéle's support of educational programs from 2005 to 2009 came from Comcel/Voilà, initially directly from the company and subsequently from the Voilà Foundation. In 2009, the parent company, Trilogy International, received an award from US Secretary of State Hillary Clinton in recognition of their support for social issues, primarily through Yéle, and their significant contribution to the economic development of Haiti.

The state of education in Haiti can only be described as tragic. But what I learned over five years of supporting the group of extraordinary NGOs that we worked with is that the expertise needed to fix the education system is already in place. Against all the odds, and facing tremendous obstacles, the seven groups we supported were making, and continue to make, a huge difference in the lives of disadvantaged young people in Haiti.

Gonaïves by bike

I coordinated a visit by Wyclef to Gonaïves in June 2005 to visit the first three of the schools that had been renovated by PADF. The visit was kept secret because we wanted to minimize the crowd situation in Gonaïves. The United Nations kindly lent us a helicopter to take Wyclef, the Yéle team and media representatives so that we would not have to make our way in what was, in those days, an extremely uncomfortable five and a half hour drive over roads that had been severely damaged by the 2004 storm.

We were at the UN base in Port-au-Prince about to take off in the helicopter, when Wyclef took me aside and said he wanted to ride a motorcycle when we arrived in Gonaïves. I explained that the UN had arranged local transport for us there and, more important, it was ten minutes before we were to take off and he had been briefed on all the arrangements prior to this and never mentioned motorcycles. However, I quickly reminded myself that Wyclef always had a good reason for asking for something, even at the last moment. I got on the phone and reached the head of Le Fonds de Parrainage National (FPN), Antoine Levelt, who was to meet us in Gonaïves. (His NGO was managing the scholarship program for Yéle, and doing an amazing job in the face of tremendous challenges.) I explained that we needed five motorcycles and that we would be landing in forty-five minutes. Unfazed, Antoine called me back in a few minutes to report that he had found five motorcycle taxi drivers who were delighted to give up their mode of transportation for a few hours in exchange for US$15 each, more than they would ever make in a day.

When we landed, Wyclef and some of the Yéle team climbed onto the waiting bikes. The rest of us piled into an open-sided troop carrier provided by the UN. The international body had gone all out for this visit and added several additional vehicles, including two white UN tanks. It suddenly made sense to me that Wyclef did not want people to see him in a UN troop vehicle, removed from them.

At the first of the three schools we visited that day, the students and staff quickly understood it was Wyclef when they met him, even though up to that point many had not recognized him without the signature dreadlocks he had cut off before our trip. The students had been told only that a delegation was arriving to see the school, and had no idea who would be included. Jubilation erupted when the students recognized their guest of honor. Wyclef unveiled a plaque and planted a tree in the courtyard and we proceeded to our next school.

Haiti may be poor, but cell phone connectivity is very prevalent. News of Wyclef's arrival had spread, and there were now hundreds of cheering people outside. Many followed us on bicycles and motorcycles as we made our way to the second school. When we emerged, there were upwards of a thousand people waiting, and again many followed us to the third and final school.

The last school on our agenda was quite some distance away, but word had spread. This school had also been told to expect a "delegation," but when we approached, we encountered a sea of humanity, possibly close to five thousand people. No vehicles could possibly get through, so all of us got out and walked through the crowd. People were crammed onto every balcony and rooftop. Gonaïves had not yet recovered from the horrors of the hurricane and floods the previous year, yet here was their hero in the flesh and they were not going to miss it.

We managed to make our way into the school, all three floors of which had been overrun by this point. Despite the crush of bodies on all sides, the mood was so joyful I didn't feel claustrophobic. When it came time to leave, I witnessed something that will stay with me for a lifetime. While we were inside, the UN convoy had pulled up in front of the school. When we came out, Wyclef proceeded on foot, walking slowly behind the last vehicle as the convoy carefully navigated the crowds. As this procession began, a small group nearby began to chant in unison "Gonaïves loves Wyclef" in Creole. It was the moment people had been waiting for: to give a collective message to Wyclef. Suddenly, what had been a handful became hundreds, chanting the same words. A tidal wave of sound moved outwards from the center as thousands more took up the chant. And as the first chant seemed to dissipate, a new one began in the center until it too moved in a wave to the outer edges. In the magic of a few minutes, all the suffering of these people was suspended and a moment of healing was taking place with Wyclef as the catalyst. The spell was broken with a final chant of "Wyclef for President" and I realized it was time to leave. I signaled the convoy to speed up and Wyclef changed his pace from walking to running. He and I were exchanging hand signals at this point, because we could not stop the convoy to consult, and thousands were running alongside and behind him.

I soon realized that we had a serious problem on our hands. About a dozen of Yéle's Haitian team were running alongside Wyclef and when we arrived at the UN base, they would not know who to let through the gates. They would see thousands of Haitians running up to the barriers and the only one they would recognize would be Wyclef.

There are times when it is helpful to be a tall, white guy and this was certainly one of them. I quickly changed vehicles, pulled ahead of the convoy, and raced to the UN base. There was no time to find the person in charge. I jumped out of the truck and quickly called the guards together. These were UN troops from various countries, but only a few were Haitians. I explained that I was now in charge and would determine who was to get through. With a mob about to descend upon them, no one argued. As the surging wall of humanity pressed at the gates, the soldiers were only too happy to let me decide who got through.

Once we were safe in the helicopter returning to Port-au-Prince, I was struck by the responsibility of what we had set in motion with Yéle. Wyclef was a unique and commanding figure in Haiti, and Yéle was an extension of him. I realized that Yéle could become, or possibly had already become, a movement that went well beyond the scope of the NGO at its center. In the following years, this became a dichotomy: organization vs. movement; and I feel we never fully came to terms with how to manage these two divergent forces. I believe Wyclef understood better than any of us that Yéle was, indeed, a movement that transcended the organization. But I was still defining Yéle by the programs that we managed.

Rice, beans, and holograms

The genesis of Yéle's new programs, following our initial focus on education, was the same for the six years I was with the organization. Wyclef would have an idea or a concern that he would share with me. I would then consult with the Yéle team, as well as other NGOs and experts in the field, and come up with a plan. After going back and forth on the details, and incorporating Wyclef's insights, a program would emerge. A good example involved food distribution in the slums. In May of 2005, Wyclef told me he was concerned about the shortage of food in the Port-au-Prince slums and felt Yéle had a responsibility to do something.

It was a time of great turmoil and instability in the country. Gangs were in control of entire slum neighborhoods such as Cité Soleil, with barricades keeping out the police and UN peacekeepers. Kidnapping was the main source of income for the gangs, and they would often attack in broad daylight and take their hostages back to the slums while they negotiated ransom payments. At night, you would hear random gunshots as the gangs implemented their warped version of justice, and in the morning, the bodies would be piled in various places where the populace would see firsthand evidence of the power of these thugs.

People living in the slums were suffering more than usual with the gangs in control, particularly when it came to food. Regular commerce had ground to a halt. The normal flow of food had become a trickle, because delivery trucks could not get through the barricades. This was the situation that concerned Wyclef, and in our first meeting to discuss the matter, I suggested approaching the World Food Programme (WFP) to seek their help.

WFP is the largest humanitarian agency in the world and gives food to an average of 90 million poor people around the globe each year. They have a long history in Haiti. Wyclef was already well known to them, because he had written a song about the flood damage in Gonaïves following Hurricane Jeanne. WFP had released it as a music video in late 2004 from their international headquarters in Rome.

I met with Guy Gauvreau (at that time Country Director of WFP Haiti) and explained that Wyclef wanted to send hip-hop musicians into Cité Soleil and other blockaded slums to distribute free food from WFP. Wyclef understood that musicians held a special status with the population and would be allowed entry when others were not, particularly if they were identified with Yéle. Guy was very happy to meet with me and enthusiastic about Wyclef's connection with WFP, but he was adamant that our proposal was completely unrealistic. WFP's last attempt to send food to Cité Soleil had been a disaster. Their truck was stopped at the barricades, the driver forced out, the contents looted, and the tires removed—all within about thirty minutes. How would Yéle be successful, when WFP, which is so well known and respected by the local population, was not?

This conversation was reported back to Wyclef, who was in Haiti at the time, and the following day he called together several local hip-hop musicians. A truck was rented and Wyclef used his own funds to purchase a quantity of rice and beans. That afternoon, the musicians drove to Cité Soleil. Wyclef was not with them, because his presence would attract crowds, making distribution impossible. But the rappers, led by a former gang member Gabriel Dorleus, known as "Killer," and hip-hop artist Jean Jimmy Alexandre, known as "Jimmy O," were allowed to enter the slum and distribute the food without incident.

The following morning I met with Guy again, this time armed with photos of the distribution that had taken place the previous day. He was surprised, and within an hour we had concluded the basic terms of a partnership between Yéle and WFP that was to last for the next five years. WFP would supply rice, beans and cooking oil which Yéle would distribute, free of charge, to poor families in the slums of Port-au-Prince.

After the first few months of distribution, it was clear that we needed to be more targeted, as some of the food was showing up for sale in local markets in the original WFP bags. In response, we settled on a two-part strategy. First, we had our own bags made locally that had both the WFP and Yéle logos and a phrase in Creole that said "free and not for sale." Wyclef had wanted the phrase to read "if someone is trying to sell this to you, hit them," but this did not get past WFP. The second part of the strategy was to introduce coupons that were exchanged for a ration of food. While this had been done previously in Haiti by WFP, we printed the coupons ourselves and restricted them to women only. I felt strongly that women would be less likely to sell the food. Although there was some resistance within our own team, and initially from the community, it ended up being widely accepted.

At first, we printed the coupons on different colored paper for each distribution to make them more difficult to counterfeit. The musicians would take the coupons into various slums, meet with the local community leaders, and determine which families were in greatest need. These families would then be given coupons. The date and location of the next distribution was written on each coupon, usually the next day. A site would be chosen and the food delivered, either the night before or early that morning. The musicians would then enlist the help of local men to manage the distribution and help with security. Only women, accompanied by children to help them carry the heavy packages, were allowed to come into the site and leave with the ration they exchanged for their coupon. This was typically a 25 kg. bag of rice (55 lbs.), a 5 kg. bag of dry beans (11 lbs.), a 1.5 liter bottle of cooking oil (just over three pints), and a small bag of salt.

The women would pile the rice and beans on their heads without hesitation. It never failed to amaze me how even frail, elderly women would hoist these huge bags onto their heads without a second thought. There was always something very graceful about the way they walked with these heavy loads on their head, how they carefully navigated the uneven mud streets, as if poised in slow motion, while all around them the world moved at full speed.

People eventually caught on to my system and forged the colored coupons, and as a result we ran out of food at a few distributions. I then found a US company that made circular half-inch diameter hologram stickers with the Yéle logo, and had them printed up cheaply in batches of 10,000. From then on, each coupon bore a hologram. Not only were there no more forgeries, but the coupons could not be used again, because each was specific for date and location.

Shortly after we began the food distribution program, Yéle gained a reputation for being able to get into difficult places and effectively deliver aid. One of the most poignant examples of this involved a helicopter reconnaissance photo taken of Cité Soleil just hours before the UN peacekeepers stormed the barricades in early February 2007, engaged in a major gun battle, and took control of the area from the gangs. The photo clearly showed an orderly lineup of people. The UN official who showed it to me, a few days after the battle, said that this was a Yéle food distribution which had taken place around 11:00am, well before the UN troops invaded that afternoon.

By the end of 2005, we were distributing food from WFP to 800 families on a regular basis. Each family received a standard "ration" of rice, beans, cooking oil, and salt. This grew over the years, and at its peak in 2008, we were supplying WFP rations to around 10,000 families a month. This expansion was only possible due to a fortuitous connection with Rob Padberg and the NGO he founded and led, the Bureau de Nutrition et Développement (BND). This exceptionally well run organization provides hot meals in schools, trains school cooks, and helps support local business cooperatives that produce food products. As they already had a foothold in the school system, BND agreed to distribute two-thirds of the food we received from WFP to the families of students in schools where they worked. We distributed the rest, using our own team, in various slums. Whether directly through Yéle, or via BND through schools, the food was distributed exclusively to women. Our partnership with BND lasted until 2009.

BND currently provides around 245,000 hot meals a day for school children in poor communities throughout Haiti, and some 45,000 of them also receive a morning snack that helps them stay alert in class. For families that find it hard to scrape together a few hot meals a week—and hardly ever on a daily basis—the service BND provides has a profound impact on keeping kids in school and helping them to concentrate on their lessons.

Clean street dignity

Yéle had begun with a focus on education at our launch in January 2005. Within months, we had added a major food distribution operation, and a few months later, embarked on what would be the highest profile program of all: street cleaning.

The combination of Wyclef's unique stature among the poor, with Yéle as the organization backing him up, had quickly become an incredible force for good in Haiti. All our programs were shaped by that dynamic in one way or another. And following the original education initiatives, each new program began in the same way, with Wyclef identifying the need and me coming up with the detailed program and finalizing it with his and Jerry's input. Included in those plans was the specific role Wyclef would play in each case.

Prior to the 2010 earthquake, our highest profile program was a classic example of this procedure. In mid-2005, Wyclef insisted that it was time for Yéle to get involved in cleaning up the streets of Port-au-Prince. I felt the idea was premature, given that we had only launched that January and had just begun the food distribution program in partnership with WFP. However, knowing that Wyclef had his finger on the pulse, I set out to find a way for us to get involved. In one of those moments that sends a chill down your spine, I had no sooner set out on this mission, than John Currelly, Country Director of the Pan American Development Foundation (PADF) and with whom we were rebuilding schools in Gonaïves, asked to meet with me.

John explained that PADF had just been approached by the U.S. government's overseas aid program, USAID, to take over and revive a failing program to employ local people to collect garbage off the streets. John felt that Yéle would be the perfect partner in the program, with PADF implementing it and Yéle serving as the brand and responsible for community relations. In a matter of days, and with Wyclef's enthusiastic blessing, we agreed on the terms of a collaboration that lasted for more than two years. Every worker wore a T-shirt with a big Yéle logo, and a smaller one representing PADF. The Yéle brand was a form of protection for the street cleaners, as many of them were working in places, such as Cité Soleil, which were still barricaded and closed to the police and UN troops.

Wyclef called the program "Pwojè Lari Pwòp" or "Project Clean Streets," with a tag line "Respect Yourself, Clean Up Your Country." He recorded a jingle for airing on radio that explained the purpose of the program, and he also recorded a mixtape for distribution to tap-taps— the highly decorated vehicles used as transport by the poor. While Wyclef was keenly aware of the power of the Yéle brand, he was equally aware of how the community felt about groups like USAID. Under his direction, I had to include in the negotiations with PADF that the USAID logo would initially not appear at all on the T-shirts or PR related to the program. This was not an easy sell, since USAID was paying for the whole operation. But Wyclef was adamant that Yéle could not launch Pwojè Lari Pwòp if USAID was identified with it. His plan, which was finally accepted and followed to the letter, was to introduce USAID in stages: at first launch, we would make no reference to them; then wait a few months before introducing a small USAID logo and only later, include a larger logo, when the community had time to get comfortable with the idea.

At its height, Pwojè Lari Pwòp employed around 2,000 people a day to clean the streets and remove garbage. The workers in their bright orange Yéle T-shirts and matching caps were seen everywhere in Port-au-Prince in those years, a huge boost for Yéle to have our brand so visible.

And for PADF, the partnership had very practical consequences. So many people signed up that they restricted workers to a four-week stint, after which the next group would be engaged. There was always a long waiting list.

There were tangible security consequences to Yéle's involvement. One particular case serves to illustrate. The workers were paid in cash in the district of the city in which they were working. This meant that payroll was taken every two weeks into places like Cité Soleil, and this involved getting gang approval to pass through the barricades. Standard protocol required the driver, security agent, and payroll manager to all wear the Yéle T-shirts of Pwojè Lari Pwòp. But on one occasion, the payroll car was seized by gang members shortly after entering Cité Soleil. The three people were detained and roughly US$20,000 in payroll was taken. PADF was alerted and they quickly informed gang leader Amaral Duclona, who also served as a team leader for one contingent of Pwojè Lari Pwòp workers. Within hours, the matter was resolved with an explanation by the notorious Amaral that a rogue gang had stolen the money because they did not know the code of conduct regarding Yéle's programs. The car, personnel, and all US$20,000 were returned to PADF. No money was withheld, even though one could easily have expected payment to be requested for arranging the return. Amaral swore he would kill the rogue gang leader as evidence of his outrage. Thankfully, he was convinced that this gesture was not necessary and his outrage would be just as convincing if he let the man live.

Garbage tunes

Wyclef soon felt we needed more than just the T-shirts, radio jingles and posters to promote Pwojè Lari Pwòp. He came up with the idea of a hip-hop competition to further popularize the program. So I soon found myself immersed in the planning and implementation of the first competition of its kind in Haiti. We enlisted the rapper Jimmy O, who was also a Yéle staff member, to be the public face of the competition.

Youth from three of the slums—Cité Soleil, the ironically named "Bel Air," and Marche Salomon—were invited to write original raps on a theme of picking up garbage from the streets and protecting the environment. Since rap music starts with lyrics, the first stage of the competition required the youth to submit their creations in writing. We formed a committee in each of the three areas made up of local musicians and community leaders, and their assignment was to choose the ten best raps in each area based on the lyrics. I insisted on two rules: first, the inclusion of a minimum of three lines of text from a list of phrases about the subject such as "eliminate the garbage, make room for cleanliness" so we could be sure the messages were to the point; second, no profane language. This was a point of some contention, but I finally convinced Jimmy O that we could not use charity funds if there were expletives in the texts. This was not entirely true, but I am uncomfortable when it comes to profanity, and I felt this was my modest contribution to improving the human condition through reducing the use of swear words.

We created flyers, posters, street banners, and radio ads to promote the competition and received hundreds of entries, due, in part, to the significant prizes. The three grand prize winners would each get 20,000 gourdes, the equivalent of about US$450.00. This was a hefty sum, considering the average daily income of US$2.00 for the poor. The three winning songs were also to be included on a special release CD on which Wyclef would have some songs. The cover of the CD would include a photo of Wyclef, and each winner was to get 300 copies of the CD to sell or give away as they wanted.

The ten semi-finalists from each area then had to perform at a concert in their community. From these three concerts, the twelve finalists were chosen. The concert in Cité Soleil had to be held just outside the barricades that still surrounded the slum, since it would have been impossible to guarantee that the sound equipment would make it back out. The concerts drew crowds of around 5,000 each. Since being a finalist would be the most important event in the life of these kids, coming as they did from such terrible slum conditions, we made up certificates for the finalists with a gold seal attaching a ribbon to the document to show our respect for them.

What really captured the imagination of these kids was that all twelve of the semi-finalist rap groups—some individuals, but most involving three or more performers—were sent to a professional studio to record their competition entry. None of them had ever seen the inside of a studio and they were incredibly excited. I was amazed to hear the professional quality of the music that emerged from the studios. But they had no idea what was about to happen.

We took the twelve raps and had Wyclef record an introduction to each, giving the name of the song, the names of the performers and a number from one to twelve. We then paid to have the songs aired on radio stations throughout Haiti for a month and a half, and the public was invited to phone in their vote for the best song. The raps were an immediate hit, and stations began playing them far more than we had contracted for because they were so popular. The airwaves were saturated with raps about cleaning the streets—noteworthy for the absence of profane language—and the twelve finalists were often in the press. The young rappers would turn up to meet the Pwojè Lari Pwòp workers on the street, media in tow, and always received a rapturous welcome. The status of the street cleaners themselves rose and they began to be interviewed and quoted, and were even asked to pose with the finalists of a national beauty pageant.

We had set up two dedicated phone lines and a staff focused only on recording the votes that were called in. We received more than 6,000 votes over the course of six weeks. This was a buildup to the final televised competition in June 2006, at which all twelve semi-finalists performed in front of a panel of four judges. The phone vote constituted the fifth "judge." There were three winners, one from each of the three neighborhoods of Cité Soleil, Bel Air, and Marche Salomon. Having one winner from each area would ensure that there would be no hard feelings between the slums, which often had issues that resulted in violent incursions into their respective territories by armed groups from the other areas.

The day before the live, televised competition I received a panicked phone call with news that the finalists were all on strike. I was stunned. What could they possibly be thinking? As it turned out, they were embarrassed because they could not afford new outfits and they wanted to look their best on television. Although they had each received 1,000 gourdes prize money (about US$25.00) at the community competition level, I had not factored in buying outfits. I quickly arranged for all of them to go to a clothing store and set up a credit line with the owner. The kids were elated as they chose their outfits—although Yéle was henceforth permanently banned from this particular store. We had not fully briefed the owner in advance as to the social status of the kids, and they were considerably more vocal and animated than the usual clientele. But that was a price I happily accepted.

A few days after the televised competition, I met with the three finalist groups. I had set up a bank account for each individual and handed them the checks with their winnings. I explained that whatever was left in the account in three months I would double, as a way to encourage them not to spend it all at once. They were stunned at this, and I was feeling rather good, thinking their silence reflected appreciation of this offer. Finally one of them, by the name of Franer, spoke up and said that what they had won was not only for themselves. He explained that they were expected to share the money with their extended family and neighbors. And because the amount of the prize had been published, everyone knew in advance exactly how much they would get! The winning rappers would get to keep only a small fraction of the money and there would certainly be nothing left in the bank in three months.

Working in Haiti was a continual learning experience for me. But my good intentions were laced with many assumptions that I did not question until faced with street reality. While it spoke to grinding poverty and the realities of life in the slums, the idea of sharing the winning money, as the rappers described, moved me deeply. In my culture, the first reaction to winning money—myself included, to be honest—would more likely be a focus on self and on others only after that. Here, sharing came first.

Time after time, I witnessed how rap music could be a tool for immense social good when harnessed appropriately.

Condoms by concert

Haiti has the highest incidence of HIV/AIDS in the Western Hemisphere and the largest number of people living with HIV/AIDS in the Caribbean. Management and Resources for Community Health (MARCH) is an NGO founded in 1985 by Dr. Tony Augustin, and the organization is a leading provider of health care in Haiti. In 2006, they were operating a network of five hospitals and sixteen health centers and dispensaries and providing HIV counseling, testing, and peer-to-peer HIV education.

It was in this context that Tony and I met. MARCH had been organizing music concerts throughout Haiti for some time to promote
awareness of HIV/AIDS and safe sex. They had some success with
these concerts using a traditional music group called TRAK, performing salsa and compas, Haiti's modern form of méringue music. But
after hearing of Yéle's success with the music competition for Pwojè
Lari Pwòp, Tony felt that hip-hop would help attract a younger audience, especially in view of the fact that youth from between ten and
twenty-four make up 26 percent of the entire Haitian population.

We asked Jimmy O to take the lead in this initiative, and he began by
enlisting seven other hip-hop musicians who committed to touring with
MARCH to add a rap component to the concerts. The first order of business was to write original hip-hop tunes about HIV/AIDS awareness and
safe sex. For that, the singers needed some education on the issues. Tony
and I agreed that the eight rappers should enroll in a two-week HIV/
AIDS peer counseling training being conducted by MARCH. Jimmy
O was reluctant to even raise this with the other musicians. It was one
thing to sing about the issue, but a two-week course seemed too close an
association with a taboo subject. I made no headway with him until I
mentioned that the other participants in the course would all be young
women. All eight rappers signed up within an hour, took the course very
seriously, and wrote brilliant raps on the subject.

There was only one slight hiccup when the Yéle rap group joined
the MARCH tour. The first concert drew an audience estimated at
more than 6,000 people, significantly more than had attended before
the addition of hip-hop to the lineup. But the huge crowd meant that
when they handed out free condoms at the end of the performance, as
was standard, they ran out in a matter of minutes. Future concerts were
well enough stocked to meet the new demand.

For almost two years, Jimmy O and the group were part of the
MARCH concert tour. They travelled the length and breadth of Haiti,
going to remote parts of the country with a message about HIV/AIDS
and safe sex. MARCH set up a mobile HIV testing unit at many concerts. An announcement was made from the stage that anyone could

volunteer to be tested free of charge and get immediate results. Those who tested positive received counseling and were referred to the nearest HIV treatment center for care.

Yéle's role was modest by comparison to MARCH, but I was struck by the real and direct health impact our rapper team had on their audiences. The potential of hip-hop to educate and introduce behavioral change in developing countries is a great untapped resource. Whereas other musical forms require expensive instruments, rap is immediate and inexpensive. Instruments enhance the music, but aside from a boom box to provide a backup beat, the punch is in the lyrics. Although I am still irritated by the posturing, violence, materialism, and machismo of hip-hop, I am dazzled by the raw power of the poetry, the direct connection to the street, and the sheer impact of rap when it takes on social issues.

I was also struck by a recurring theme at the heart of everything we did in Haiti. Despite the social, political and economic turmoil that came in successive waves, month after month and year after year, the NGO community was able to introduce innovations without hindrance, because the country was not organized enough to coordinate interference or put up bureaucratic hurdles. In this case, neither could the church, which had so long resisted the use of condoms in other developing countries. This freedom was both good and bad: good in that, as with HIV/AIDS, the innovations introduced by NGOs such as MARCH were tailored to Haiti's specific needs and resulted in an overall decline in HIV infection rates among men and women aged fifteen to forty-nine from 3.8 percent in 2005 to 2.2 percent by the end of 2008, according to UNAIDS. But it was bad in that the government did not play a direct role in such a vital health issue. Ultimately, NGO interventions will be limited in their lasting impact unless reinforced by a well functioning government. The percentage of infection did come down and Haiti now has the second highest rate of HIV infection in the region. It will remain at that level, however, until the government gets involved. Years of solid NGO successes in one sector can still be undone with lightning speed by the next wave of turmoil and social upheaval that is a way of life in Haiti.

Name tags and spirits

Throughout Haiti, particularly in slums like Cité Soleil, Vodou is a strong presence and the source of a myriad of myths. Originally brought by African slaves, it represents a uniquely Haitian belief system and religious practice for the majority of Haitians, especially the very poor, incorporating many beliefs and practices from West Africa. Catholicism may rank higher in census statistics, but does not accurately reflect day-to-day reality. Many who identify themselves as Catholics, or follow other Christian traditions, also practice Vodou in some form.

I attended my first Vodou ceremony in the autumn of 2005. With a couple of friends, I set out late one night for Croix-des-Bouquets, a suburb of Port-au-Prince well known for both Vodou and metal sculptors. These artisans work almost exclusively in iron, much of it originating as iron drums. We had been invited by a Vodou hougan, or priest, named Pierre-Richard Desrosiers, also a metal sculptor by day.

The trip itself was somewhat dangerous, as we took no security agent or guns—despite the frequent reports of kidnappings. But since I was with friends who had lived for many years in the country and knew their way around, I figured it was safe enough.

We arrived around 11:00 p.m., through a courtyard thronged with people, and entered the temple, a building that had been built to serve as a Vodou house of worship or "hounfour." We were warmly welcomed by Pierre-Richard, although we were clearly the only foreigners in the midst of what seemed to be several thousand Haitians. Pierre-Richard was at pains to make us comfortable and we were free to go anywhere at any time during the ceremony. The building was arranged around a large, two-story central space, with a large red post rising the full two stories in the middle. It was explained that this post was used during ceremonies to attract spirits into the temple.

Christian images of St. George and the Dragon, Moses and the Ten Commandments, and the Virgin Mary, all white-skinned, shared the walls of the main floor with various Vodou figures. I had been told that Vodou theology centers on one God, referred to as Bondyè, but their worship is mainly directed at the many subordinate deities, which include Catholic saints.

I was fascinated to see that many of the worshipers wore color-coded name tags. Pierre-Richard explained that the people who were attending this important ceremony had come from many different Vodou groups in the region. The colored tags identified the community they came from. That this religion, so rooted in unfathomable mystery and ritual, would utilize a computer program to generate color-coded name tags encased in plastic was one of those delightful moments of humorous duality. And of course my own preconceived notion about Vodou was given a healthy reality check.

The ceremony began with several dozen men and women, many dressed in white and wearing white head scarves, dancing in the central space around the red pole. Pierre-Richard left briefly and came back with a platter of chicken, rice, and beans. We had seen this platter on an alter during our earlier tour and I remember thinking that it looked rather unsanitary, with hordes of flies buzzing around it. Now it appeared that, in his capacity as priest, Pierre-Richard was taking this same platter around the room and inviting people to use their hands to take a portion and eat it. My friends were safely at the back at this point, but I was in the central space taking in the action. Anxious not to be rude by refusing this offering, but also not to get sick, I kept moving around the central pillar to shield myself from Pierre-Richard as he passed through with the platter. Thankfully, I was not spotted.

He seemed to go into a trance and I was told that he had been possessed by an evil spirit. My rudimentary understanding of the tradition was that if a bad spirit was identified, steps would be taken to transform it into a good spirit.

Many worshippers now moved into a tight group on one side of the central open space. As I ventured closer, I saw that the congregation had dug a hole in the dirt floor the size and proportions of a bathtub, and sitting in it was Pierre-Richard, holding a wooden pole the size of a walking stick. Water was poured on the stick, and people were chanting and shouting vigorously, their attention riveted on both the priest and the stick. Someone said that Pierre-Richard had tricked an evil spirit into going under the stick. Suddenly, he jumped out of the hole and the congregation immediately filled the opening and packed down the earth until all that was left was the top of the stick. I was assured that after two weeks of daily prayer, the evil spirit that was trapped beneath the stick would be transformed into a good one and released.

The ceremony continued with dancing, singing, and chanting. I wandered about, taking it all in, with everyone showing kindness and welcoming my presence. While I understood little of what was taking place, I felt honored to witness Vodou in operation. It has an impact on every aspect of daily life in Haiti and is a subtle presence in the political, social and economic life of the country. You cannot work in Haiti without at least acknowledging the role of Vodou.

After the ceremony my three friends and I roamed the streets of Croix-des-Bouquets. By the light of a full moon, without street lights, it felt strange to just wander like this, conditioned as we all were to being constantly surrounded by security personnel and forbidden to be on the streets without the protection of guns. Now, well past midnight, we encountered few people on the street. Passing a couple of bakeries bustling with activity, we went into one, just as a pan of fresh rolls was being removed from the oven. The owner welcomed us warmly and offered us samples. We waited a minute for the steaming rolls to cool and then bit into the soft, aromatic bread for a culinary experience that will stay with me forever.

Head-of-state protocol

A distinctly different culinary experience took place in September 2006, when I organized a private dinner in Toronto for Wyclef to meet then Governor General of Canada, Michaëlle Jean. I felt it was important that two of the highest profile public figures of Haitian descent in North America should become acquainted, my choice more than a little influenced by pride in my Canadian heritage.

Earlier in the day I had met with Wyclef to discuss the dinner, and to explain who the Governor General was—not an easy concept for a non-Canadian. While Canada is a parliamentary democracy with an elected prime minister, it is also a constitutional monarchy, whose head of state, Queen Elizabeth II, is represented in Canada by the Governor General. I had laid out a selection of Canadian coins and bills, with the profile of the Queen facing up, and explained to Wyclef that this lady is held in such high esteem by all Canadians that we put her on all our money. I went on to explain that the woman he was to meet that evening was the Queen's representative. He was to address the Governor General as "Your Excellency," and afterwards as "Madam." I was concerned that Wyclef would lapse into his usual informality, and I wanted to make sure he took the whole thing very seriously.

Because he was serving as host, Wyclef was to stand at the door and greet Her Excellency and the other guests, and once seated, he would have to give a toast to the guest of honor. He looked askance at this last suggestion, and I realized this was not part of his background. So we practiced the toast several times: when he was to stand, when the guests would stand, how to hold the glass by the stem so that the sound of the clinking glasses would ring, how to word the toast.

That night you would have thought Wyclef had done this all his life. He was always a quick study, and trusted me to guide him in these situations. I stood next to him at the entrance to the room and whispered the name of each guest as they arrived so that he could greet them. I had chosen a few key figures from the business and communication field so that we could potentially follow up with them later for Yéle. There were nineteen people seated around the table. At the right moment, I nodded to Wyclef that it was time for the toast, and he carried it off with faultless panâche.

We had a delightful conversation with Her Excellency, who had been briefed in advance on the work of Yéle. She had been born in Port-au-Prince before emigrating to Canada as a refugee in 1968. During the evening she told us of a project she was undertaking to promote youth leadership and development in Canada, and asked if there was a way we might be able to assist her. It so happened that we were planning a concert for the southern resort city of Jacmel that December, so by the end of dinner we had worked out a plan for her to choose ten young Canadians to travel to Haiti for that event.

The Governor General was both elegant and regal, and at the same time, friendly and approachable—not an easy combination to pull off—illustrating the inherent nobility of the Haitian people that I had come to appreciate.

And she did something delightfully thoughtful at the end of dinner when we were saying goodbye. She had been briefed about Yéle and also about the program my mother, Mikky Locke, then eighty years old and living in the province of Alberta, had created for Canadian schoolchildren to give 25 cents each towards scholarships to enable poor children in Haiti to attend school through Yéle. Her Excellency asked me to give two messages to my mother: first, to thank her for what she was doing for the children of Haiti, and second, for raising me to do what I was doing for the people of her native country. As you might imagine, my mother was transported to another dimension when she received this message from the representative of the Queen.

Music on the beach

Wyclef had long wanted to mount a large concert in Haiti, to send a message to Haitians that the country was stable enough to host a large event. Other than the annual Carnival celebrations, there had been no large entertainment of this kind for several years and Wyclef understood the symbolic importance such an event would have on the national psyche.

In mid-2006 we were just beginning to explore a partnership for a different project with David Belle and the Jacmel Film Festival. Wyclef agreed that we should combine forces with David and hold the first "YéleFest" to coincide with their film festival in the seaside city of Jacmel—away from the security nightmare that was Port-au-Prince. Linking YéleFest to a serious film festival would lend gravitas and focus; and, on a practical level, Yéle needed the help of an established organization to help with logistics. The result was one of the most amazing and rewarding events of my career: YéleFest, which took place in early December 2006.

While both Jacmel and Port-au-Prince are on the ocean, most of the waterfront of Port-au-Prince consists of either slums, like Cité Soleil, or port facilities, themselves surrounded by slums. There are no parks or beaches that the general public can enjoy. By contrast, Jacmel, with its sparkling water and sandy beaches, open to all, is reminiscent of the French Riviera. Granted, the hotels are rundown, echoing a once-glamorous past, but their faded glory has its own appeal. There were even several great restaurants nearby, where wealthier residents of Port-au-Prince had weekend beach houses. Jacmel is also known for its painters, sculptors, artisans, and a long tradition of making intricate papier-mâché masks for the annual Carnival celebration.

The centerpiece of our collaboration with the film festival was a large stage on the beach. David and I had decided that we would build the concert stage and have it up early so that it could double as the venue for outdoor film screenings leading up to the Wyclef concert as the finale. A simple idea, but the devil was in the details.

Reality check: there were no world-class portable stages, sound and lighting systems, large video screens and the other paraphernalia for mounting such a concert in Haiti; there was not enough electricity in Jacmel to run such an operation, and no building large enough to host the VIPs we wanted to invite. Undaunted, David and I joined forces with Wyclef's resourceful and efficient tour manager, Charmant Noncent, and found a staging company in the Dominican Republic which, after considerable coaxing and assurances that Jacmel did not pose the same security risk as Port-au-Prince, agreed to truck everything in. Not until I stood on the beach and saw the immensity of the whole thing under construction did the scale of the enterprise become real. The stage itself was enormous, with metal trusses on both sides rising fifty feet in the air. Several video screens were installed, so that the crowd, which would stretch out along the eighty-foot-wide strip of beach, would have a good view. A multistory control tower was built in the audience area, and a 100-foot catwalk extended out from the stage. An elevator would bring Wyclef from underneath the stage at the appropriate moment. It took several days for the fifteen-member Dominican setup crew, matched by a local crew of twenty, to complete the installation.

But where to house the VIPs and special guests? We had already booked every hotel and guesthouse in the area, rented several large vacant homes, and taken over every room in the beachfront Jacmelienne Hotel as our headquarters. What we needed was a VIP reception area near the stage. So we decided to approach the owner of the hotel with an offer he could not refuse: Yéle would pay for the construction, on open land next to the hotel, of a very large pavilion that would then belong to the hotel afterwards at no cost. David and I designed a traditional, open-sided Haitian *choucoune* with a thatched roof supported by poles, large enough to seat up to 100 people at tables. A local construction company secured the palm branches for the roof, eventually supplied by many small farmers along the coast. Guests who saw the magnificent final structure, with its soaring interior open rafters supporting the thatched roof, assumed it had been there for years, although it was completed only the day before they arrived.

The collaboration between Yéle and the Film Festival focused on a series of documentaries on a range of issues such as violence against women, HIV/AIDS, and the environment, each followed by a seminar. Yéle invited NGO, government ministry, and UN representatives to participate in panel discussions after each screening. The environment, for example, was covered by a screening of Al Gore's film "An Inconvenient Truth" about global warming. We did not know whether the general public would be interested in these subjects, but were heartened to have standing room only and spirited interactions between the audience and panelists following each film.

Canadian Governor General Michaëlle Jean had asked whether Wyclef would work with her youth leadership program and sponsor ten young Canadians to come to Haiti in connection with YéleFest. We decided to link these youth with a local art school and several local artists, led by a prominent abstract artist named Ronald Mevs. Added to this creative mix was a local Jacmel couple, Paule and Moro

Baruk. Consultation among this extended group generated the idea to have the Canadian youth work with a similar number of local art students, guided and assisted by the older established artists, to design and build a sculpture that incorporated papier mâché carnival masks, to be burned in a ceremony at the midpoint of Wyclef's concert. The idea of burning the sculpture arose from the fact that carnival masks made locally are often burned after being worn, so that the spirit of the creature portrayed in the mask will not haunt the wearer.

Like many creative ideas, this was both captivating and logistically challenging. We had to sink wooden piles into the floor of the ocean to hold the sixty-foot pier and platform, so that the sculpture could burn without harming anyone, but still be close enough to be seen. The students were assisted by the local artists to find supplies, and the artists also served as consultants for the physical construction of the sculpture. The students had several days to come up with the design. What they presented was nothing short of fantastical. They proposed a wooden tower on the platform, topped by a huge drum on which the oversize carnival masks would be placed. They also wanted the ceremonial burning of the sculpture to be preceded by fireworks which would shoot out from the base of the tower. After overcoming my initial shock and an auto-response regarding budget overruns, I realized that we had to honor the creative spirit behind this and agreed to the whole enterprise. My side of the bargain involved some highly creative budgeting.

We called it the "Falla Boucon," which translates loosely as "burning sculpture."

The beach-side stage, pier and platform were built simultaneously. In the midst of the chaos of concert preparations, I met often with the students and local artists, who were all incredibly focused and worked long hours to realize their design. On the day of the concert, the tower was installed and with only hours to spare, the drum with the attached masks went up. On paper it had looked beautiful, but in reality, the elegant tower topped by the huge drum was dazzling in its intensity of color and shape. Long strips of cloth, attached to the drum and echoing its colors, completed the artistic expression. The ocean breeze transformed each strip into a moving sculptural element, with the whole creation hovering over the water as if by magic.

On the day of the concert, tens of thousands of people streamed into Jacmel. We mounted a huge security operation, although there had been no intimation that it would be needed. Two hundred UN peace-keeping (MINUSTAH) troops were brought in and deployed around the town, along with 100 national police from Port-au-Prince—all this on top of our private security team of about twenty-five. The evening came off without a single incident.

Moments before the concert, I was standing with my wife, April, on the viewing platform we had built for VIPs adjacent to the stage—the first moment I was able to take it all in. Before us was a crowd of some 80,000 people. No matter how confident I can be in my work, there are moments when I am in awe of what I am privileged to be part of. This was one of those transcendent moments.

Wyclef had invited several Haitian artists to perform before he came on stage. He was always deeply respectful of local talent, and on this, as on so many other occasions, he gave up a lot of stage time so that others could be profiled. There was no mistaking when Wyclef made his entrance, however, as this involved getting a horse on stage.

Wyclef had decided to come on stage with an actor dressed as Toussaint Louverture, the legendary leader of the Haitian Revolution. In keeping with this theme, he and the actor were to arrive on stage on horseback. We finally procured a horse, but it came without a handler. Consequently, I found myself joining another colleague trying to prod the poor beast up the steps leading to the stage without getting kicked.

Wyclef put on an amazing show. I was backstage, keeping an eye on the schedule, when suddenly I heard him call my name. I walked backstage to a point where we could make eye contact, assuming there was something he needed done backstage. Instead, he motioned for me to come out. I thought this meant he had instructions to whisper to me. As I walked toward him, he addressed the audience in Creole and mentioned my name. As I approached, he explained that he was going to speak to the audience and then translate for me. He told them that I was the executive director of Yéle Haiti, and then asked if they wanted to hear me speak Creole, to which the audience roared back in the affirmative. When I nervously explained that I did not speak any Creole, Wyclef, ever the ham in such situations, said he would break it down into phrases for me to repeat. I later learned that my first public speaking engagement in Creole consisted of stating that "I like rice, beans and kalalou," the latter being Creole for "okra." For days after that, people would burst out laughing, calling out "kalalou" whenever they saw me on the street.

As the highlight of the concert, Wyclef lit a torch on stage and passed it to a runner, who went through the crowd onto the pier and out to the Falla Boucon sculpture. The audience was riveted in silent anticipation. The runner lit a fuse and in seconds the fireworks exploded from the base, illuminating the sculpture. Just as the fireworks died down, flames erupted at the base of the sculpture and within minutes the whole construction was in flames, shooting 100 feet in the air.

I didn't relax until the morning after the concert. But this was Haiti, and the potential for melodrama is like a subtle mist that can take solid form when you least expect it. I was at my hotel, when a call came from a woman who had been working closely with me on the logistics for YéleFest. She was being physically detained by the owner of the Jacmelienne Hotel, who refused to release her until we had paid our bill in full. Like an episode out of the pages of a Graham Greene novel: owner of faded resort hotel holds charity representative ransom, and demands cash in a paper bag. We had a contract with the hotel and had already made two substantial wire transfers to their bank account; the contract specified that the third and final payment was due two weeks after the concert. In addition, we had cleaned up the hotel grounds and built the choucoune structure for the VIPs, at no cost to the hotel. I decided to call the police and report a kidnapping. When they asked if guns had been deployed, I pretended that the phone line was so bad that I was unable to confirm or deny the absence of firepower. I also called the mayor, Edo Zenny, who had been a great ally and supporter.

As I arrived, police swarmed the hotel, sirens blaring, guns drawn. Thankfully, Edo arrived at the same moment and took charge of the situation. He convinced the owner to release my Yéle colleague and abide by the terms of the contract that he had signed. I agreed not to press charges—tempting as that was. But this was a poignant reminder of something I encountered often in Haiti: people not trusting in deferred gratification. Some cash in hand is almost always better than more cash paid in installments down the road; a written contract is never to be trusted.

Cinema under the stars

During the course of YéleFest, we formally launched Yéle Cinema in partnership with David Belle and the Jacmel Film Festival. This partnership involved purchasing and customizing a truck with a built-in generator, sound system, and projector that would travel throughout the slums of Port-au-Prince, showing free outdoor projections of Creole-dubbed and French-language feature films and documentaries. This had been done before in Haiti, but we felt it could be taken to a new level with funding that would make it independent of commercial sponsorship and permit public service announcements and short promotional videos to address social, environmental, and economic issues.

Only one-third of households in Haiti have electricity, and even fewer families own a television. One commercial cinema was operating in the whole country at that time, and it was subsequently destroyed in the 2010 earthquake. Moreover, close to half the adult population is illiterate. It was clear to me that using popular films to attract audiences, and then interspersing them with social messages, was a great way to access a mass, otherwise hard-to-reach audience

With funding from the Government of France, we were ready to begin by the end of 2006. David's organization provided the films from their large library of Haitian and dubbed foreign films, and also agreed to operate the truck and manage the film projection. Yéle's team was responsible for logistics, choosing the locations, hiring local youth for setup, security, and cleanup. Because youth were hired from the neighborhood of each showing, we had not one single security incident. Another important Yéle contribution was to have Wyclef film an introduction to each showing as a way to convey a social message. So, for example, if a film involved Kung Fu, the message from Wyclef included a call to exercise self-discipline in connection with martial arts. For a film in which the central figure had AIDS, the message was about safe sex. A film in which the heroine was attacked by her husband called for a message about domestic violence. Wyclef knew exactly how to relate to his audience, and each of the video introductions was funny, irreverent, and thought-provoking. We were also able to get a range of PSAs and short videos about social issues, and ran these regularly before and after the feature films.

Yéle Cinema was showing films four or five nights a week and targeting twelve different poor neighborhoods throughout Port-au-Prince. Crowds of up to 6,000 people came out each night and were wildly enthusiastic, particularly when seeing Haitian-made films. Audiences in Haiti are very vocal when watching films, applauding and shouting support for the good guys, and booing and hissing the bad guys. There are animated discussions, held at a very high decibel, regarding plot developments and the motivation of various characters. Viewing films there is a social and interactive experience, and at least half the entertainment value involves the audience itself.

We ran out of funding for the program after close to a year of operation, and then started up again for several months the following year. But eventually, Yéle Cinema closed down permanently. The Jacmel Film Festival, renamed the Ciné Institute, provides world class film and media training for youth, and has emerged in recent years as a voice for Haitian cinema internationally.

Together for Haiti

In early 2008, Haiti was hit by what was dubbed the "global food crisis." Food prices had been building steadily in developing countries over several years, but spiked dramatically in one year, when rice went up 74 percent, corn by 31 percent, and wheat by 130 percent, according to the UN Food and Agriculture Organization (FAO). When a family spends from half to three-quarters of its income on food—the case for the poor in many developing countries, including Haiti—this scale of increase spells disaster. Protest riots erupted throughout Haiti in March and April of 2008. UN peacekeepers fired rubber bullets and tear gas to control demonstrations in several cities. Windows were smashed, shops looted, and cars burned. Day after day, I watched smoke from burning tires rise in ominous plumes above Port-au-Prince. A new phrase became popular: Haitians referred to their hunger pangs as "eating Clorox," because the burning in their stomachs felt like ingesting bleach.

It was obvious that Yéle had to step up our existing program of distributing free food provided by the World Food Programme (WFP). But, with my background in a farming community in rural Canada, I was also concerned to use this crisis to reach out to smallholder farmers. And while we were at it, I thought this was also the occasion to draw together several other NGOs and UN agencies to forge a new model for collaboration. Out of this came an experiment called "Together for Haiti," in which Yéle formed a coalition of like-minded organizations to mount a joint operation that would provide food, create agriculture-related jobs, and support smallholder farmers.

Even Yéle's most ardent supporters would characterize "Together for Haiti" as a failure. Despite the valuable lessons learned, we did not accomplish what we set out to do.

The partners I enlisted for Together for Haiti included the World Food Programme (WFP), the Pan American Development Foundation (PADF), and the Bureau de Nutrition et Développement (BND). The UNDP being then unpopular in Haiti, it became the silent partner: they would raise the majority of the funds and, by mutual agreement, their role would be kept quiet. In early May 2008, all the partners signed a formal agreement outlining how we would work together. Wyclef and his popular musician friend, Michel Martelly, were to serve as the public face of the operation. Martelly was then known by his stage name "Sweet Micky," while he is now addressed as "Mr. President." The President of Haiti, that is.

Together for Haiti looked good on paper. The work of the partners overlapped, justifying increased collaboration to bring more awareness to, and more funding for, our shared activities. Yéle was the lynchpin that connected them all. We held a high-profile launch in New York City, where Wyclef was joined on stage by Paul Simon and economist Jeffrey Sachs. We then ran pilot projects to demonstrate the usefulness and practicality of our collective efforts to provide food, create jobs in the agricultural sector, and support smallholder farmers.

The food part involved significantly expanding the distribution of free food. Yéle had previously been distributing food from WFP to an average of 800 families on a regular basis, primarily vulnerable families in the slums of Port-au-Prince and the surrounding area. Now, joining forces with the Bureau de Nutrition et Développement (BND), we stepped it up and took on the task of distributing 670 metric tons of WFP food to 10,000 families over the course of one year.

The agriculture and job component centered on the Pan American Development Foundation (PADF), the NGO with which Yéle had previously collaborated on the street-cleaning program. Our plan was to reestablish a similar operation, but this time have workers focus on activities that would help improve agriculture through rebuilding irrigation systems, improving rural roads, and planting shelterbelts. Great idea, but we could not raise enough money to mount a pilot operation.

However, we did manage to raise enough money to run a pilot with PADF for a program to support smallholder farmers. The idea was to give small grants and training to low-income farmers so they could increase local food production and processing, including eggs, vegetables, grain milling, and bread. To launch it, Wyclef would hand over small cages, each with a couple of egg-bearing chickens, to twelve farmers, so they could begin selling eggs. As we were preparing for a ceremonial handing over of the cages, several of them flew open and the birds got loose. Chickens can run surprisingly fast when sensing an imminent return to incarceration. By the time they were back in their cages, we were all in fits of laughter, and had to fight to keep it together enough to make the press announcement.

Another group of smallholder farmers were delighted when Wyclef presented them with high yield, non-hybrid seeds to improve their crop yields. Wyclef got quite a surprise when he recognized one of the farmers as he handed him a bag of seed; the farmer was a childhood neighbor, who had been known locally to have a particularly well dressed scarecrow that kept birds off his land.

Together for Haiti did succeed in distributing food to families in need, whereas the program to create jobs to support agriculture never got off the ground. The plans to support smallholder farmers through small grants, training, and the provision of high-quality crop seeds unfortunately did not make it past the pilot stage for lack of funding.

So what went wrong? First, I had thought—wrongly—that a good program, high-profile announcement, and solid partners would attract funding. UNDP approached several donor governments, while I reached out to foundations and philanthropies. All to no avail. I learned never to go public with something on this scale without being sure in advance that there is at least some of the funding in the bank.

But even if the funding had been in place, there was a more fundamental reason that Together for Haiti did not work: none of the partners, Yéle included, was willing to leave their respective comfort zones and enter into a partnership that was more than the sum of its parts. Yéle was the ringmaster, but none of the other partners had any real sense of ownership and responsibility for our collective initiative. By early August, it was clear that Together for Haiti had failed. A few farmers had received chickens and seeds, and we expanded the food distribution we had already been doing with WFP. But the rest of the programs did not materialize.

However, one lasting impact would be felt several years later. This brief exposure to the concerns of smallholder farmers had profoundly affected me, and I was determined to find a way to help them. I had no way of knowing that this experience would lead to one of the largest programs Yéle would ever undertake, and then to the creation of a new

NGO that would become the focus of my ongoing career in humanitarian service. Something deep inside the boy from a farming community in Saskatchewan, Canada, was awakened in the man who began working with the farmers of Haiti.

Storm quartet

If the global food crisis was the perfect storm in terms of agriculture, what followed was the real deal in terms of weather. Haiti was hit by a horrific tropical storm and three hurricanes in less than a month, beginning in August 2008. The names Fay, Gustav, Hanna, and Ike came to be reviled in Haiti, as each successive storm wrought extensive damage throughout the length and breadth of the country. This storm quartet knocked out bridges, washed away roads, destroyed homes and killed more than 500 people. Some remote communities were completely inaccessible for weeks and supplies had to be dropped by helicopter.

Hardest hit was Gonaïves, Haiti's fourth largest city. They had only just recovered from the extensive damage caused by Hurricane Jeanne in September 2004. It was the same scenario all over again, except much worse this time: the rivers that flow through Gonaïves into the ocean all broke their banks as rain poured down mountainsides long ago denuded of tree cover.

I was able to get to Gonaïves by helicopter shortly after the last storm subsided. I was shocked at the scale of the damage. Gonaïves was not simply flooded; it was a moving river, with three-quarters of the city poking up through a sea of brown water that ranged from a foot to 6 feet deep. I travelled in a UN military truck with huge wheels capable of navigating the water. We proceeded slowly down the streets, accompanied by people making their way through the moving water, often carrying heavy loads on their head or children on their backs. The currents were strong and everyone moved in slow motion for fear of stepping into a hole or obstacle. The scene had the surreal feeling of a film running at the wrong speed.

Throughout the city, people were camped on rooftops, mostly one- or two-story cement structures with flat roofs. Residents had carried up beds, furniture, and clothing, and some had strung up sheets or tarps for protection against the alternating sun and rain. It was as if a huge refugee camp had been suspended above the water.

I had come to assess what Yéle could do to help, as well as to plan for a visit by Wyclef and actor Matt Damon a few days later. They were coming to view the situation first hand with the goal of helping to generate both international attention and funding for the massive humanitarian effort underway by the government of Haiti, UN agencies, the NGO community, and various donor governments.

Within a few days, I was back in Gonaïves with Wyclef, Matt and several journalists. We flew in by UN helicopter and moved around the city in an open-sided UN transport vehicle. First, Wyclef and Matt helped with a WFP food distribution, handing out bags of rice and beans to families who had been flooded out of their homes. Then, in the central plaza, which resembled an island, Wyclef addressed a large crowd of people, who were clearly thrilled to have their hero visit them in time of need. We went to other areas of the city to see the devastation first hand, walking through the water wearing knee-high boots.

As we moved through the city, dozens of desperate people pressed close to Wyclef and handed him bits of paper with their name and cell phone numbers, clearly seeing the transfer of this tiny paper as their best hope for assistance. Wyclef would collect them all and quietly hand them to me. This was the scene everywhere he went in Haiti. People wanted jobs or assistance and knew that Yéle was active in the community. But it became more frenetic in crisis areas. I would pass the slips of paper to the Yéle team to follow up. Sadly, we were not in a position to expand our existing programs and could help only a small number.

We also travelled to Cabaret, a city of 60,000 not far from Port-au-Prince. Next to Gonaïves, they had been hardest hit by the storms and had suffered extensive damage and loss of life. Wyclef and Matt took part in two emergency relief efforts, a soup kitchen and a food distribution, being conducted jointly with our longtime partner, the Bureau de Nutrition et Développement (BND).

Our first stop was the food distribution. The plan was to have our large Yéle truck bring supplies of dry rice and beans into the courtyard of a local clinic where, once unloaded, we could conduct an orderly distribution to 200 pre-registered families, letting a few people in at a time to the enclosed space. As we arrived, we learned that the Yéle truck had been stuck in deep mud not far from the clinic and could not move despite strenuous efforts by many. We reached the spot and Wyclef and Matt waited in the vehicle while Rob Padburg, Director General of BND, and I set out to find out what was going on. The truck was stable, but definitely not going anywhere. The more pressing problem was how to conduct the distribution in the open—always a risky endeavor that can sometimes lead to a riot.

More than 600 people had gathered, not knowing that Wyclef was in the vehicle. But the moment they learned who had arrived, I knew there was likely to be jubilation, but perhaps not sufficient to prevent a riot if we opened up the truck. So without a word about Wyclef, Rob and I got the crowd to divide up into two lines of men and women, with the men forming a human chain attached at each end to the back of the truck forming an enclosure. We positioned the women in a line outside of this enclosure. Finally, Wyclef and Matt emerged. After the cheering died down, Wyclef explained that there was not enough food in the truck for everyone, but that we would provide one bag of rice and beans to as many of the women as possible.

As the truck's rear door was raised, the crowd surged forward at the sight of food. Thankfully, the human chain held. I let one woman through at a time, as Wyclef, Matt, and the Yéle and BND teams put a bag of rice and beans on each person's head. The scene was chaotic and the cheers were deafening as each woman received her allotted food. The area behind the truck was churned into a sea of mud. But it all worked. When the last bag was handed out there were still at least 50 women in the line. Wyclef again addressed the crowd and explained that once the Yéle truck had been dug out, we would return later in the day with more food. That people remained calm was a testament to both Wyclef's standing in the community and the fact that Yéle and

BND were well known and seen as reliable.

From the site of the distribution, we walked the half mile to the soup kitchen that BND was operating with food supplied by Dutch Caritas/CORDAID, a donor NGO. The kitchen had been set up in a church; each day, local people would bring their own plates to take away a hot meal. Today, all was ready for the regular operation, but we closed the church until Wyclef and Matt were inside, in the company of a handful of frail, elderly people whose homes had been washed away. Most were lying on the floor on blankets, too weak to move. When Wyclef came in, he knelt down, tenderly took each one by the hand, and spoke words of encouragement.

Wyclef and Matt readied themselves behind the huge pots to serve the rice and a hearty goat stew. The doors were opened and people filed in with their plates. When the first few people served looked askance as they walked away, I realized that Matt had not been dipping the ladle deeply enough into the pot to include any meat in the portion. This minor correction was made and everyone went away happy.

In my professional career I have enlisted a great many public figures and celebrities in support of the humanitarian work I was engaged in. They tend to fit into two broad categories: easy going and genuinely interested in the cause at hand, vs. high-maintenance, distractible, well attended, and focused on the cause only when the cameras are turned on. Matt was definitely of the first sort. He travelled without a manager or assistant and had come to Haiti as an ambassador for the ONEXONE Foundation from Canada, an early supporter of Yéle's work. Matt was clearly there to learn about the situation and was always asking questions and taking a real interest in what was going on.

Dance of the donors

For two weeks following their trip, Wyclef and Matt were in the U.S. conducting extensive TV, radio, and print interviews, appealing urgently for funds to support the American and other government contributions to the UN's emergency call to help Haiti recover from the storms.

The UN appeal failed to reach anything like its fundraising goal.

So the various donor governments, UN agencies, and international financial institutions gathered in Washington, DC in April 2009 and pledged US$392 million to help Haiti recover from the events of 2008—the food crisis, the four storms, and a great deal of political tumult. It was the first time I had attended an event of this kind, and was fascinated by what went on.

Donor conferences that convene after major disasters, regardless of which country is to be the recipient of the global largesse, follow a set pattern rather like a formal courtship conducted in public. Almost everyone involved in allocating aid is genuinely concerned with providing help, but, equally true, they are almost all forced, at one time or another, to defer to their respective bureaucracies. In following established protocols for these conferences, the donors are like suitors and the eligible virgin is the poor country that has suffered a disaster—Haiti, in this case. The poor country would seem to be the focus of the courtship, but in reality the suitors are actually courting the media at home to ensure that voters are suitably impressed with the gift being offered to win the virgin.

These gifts can be broken down into four distinct categories that apply to donor countries and disaster funding. Not every country utilizes all four categories for every disaster, but all four were evident at the donor conference for Haiti.

First, certain donor countries took some of their existing development grants for Haiti and changed a few paragraphs regarding how the funds were to be used. By this simple process, a handful of existing, already approved grants, with money still due to be paid out, were recycled and re-emerged as "new" grants. Each suitor wants to give the most munificent gift, but the goal is to do so without actually having to put too much new money on the table.

The second category of donor money is what the donor government will use to repay itself for in-kind gifts. This includes items such as food, where the donor government gives rice, for example, and then repays itself for the rice, but then announces both the rice and the repayment for the rice as part of the gift. Depending on your point of view, this counts as either double entry or strategic accounting.

Third on the list is new money, almost always less than half of the total gift and sometimes as little as a third. It will be the only money which is actually intended to get through and be disbursed, and which is not part of a recycled grant or support which arrives as an in-kind gift for which the donor government will later reimburse itself.

The final category is money which the donor government will never have to pay, but which helps to increase the size of the gift when it is announced at the conference. They will never have to actually pay this money out because it is tied to conditions that no recipient government could ever live up to. At first glance, each condition looks as if it describes government procedures or economic policy. But, upon closer inspection, is wholly inappropriate to the target recipient, which is hard pressed to point this out for fear of jeopardizing the rest of the gift. Moreover, no other donor government will blow the whistle, because they all play the same game at one time or another.

When the period of public courtship is declared over near the close of the conference, each donor country stands and announces their gift, eliciting varying decibels of applause depending on the dollar amount. National media take note of their country's pledge and duly report it to voters back home. With the complicit agreement of everyone involved—including the media who are in on the scheme—all participants know that the full amount will never be paid out. The media will make the appropriate protests of indignation when reporting a year later to say that the funds were not paid in full, but eventually the story will fade, and the full amount pledged will never be seen.

Of the US$392 million pledged at the Haiti Donors' Conference in April 2009, less than one third had been disbursed a year later. Beyond that time, all the donors were off the hook for this conference because they were, quite reasonably, dealing with the earthquake that struck in January 2010. But the same courtship ritual played out in response to donor money in response to the earthquake, including some of the US$392 million that was recycled as new.

Absolution by audit

I would be remiss, while pointing a finger at donors for their monetary dealings, if I did not discuss Yéle's challenges in this regard.

There were two big infusions of cash into Yéle Haiti in 2006, one a private donation, and the other a fundraising event held in Monte Carlo. After receiving this money, three Yéle financial transactions were to capture the headlines years later, because they were made to companies controlled by Wyclef and Jerry, both members of Yéle's board of directors. When a charity makes payments to a board member for services, regardless of their nature, it is termed a "related party transaction," and must be declared as such, so that the IRS can ensure that the proper rules for such transactions are followed. Accordingly, Yéle declared these three items as related party transactions in our IRS tax filings.

The first of the three transactions involved a fee paid by Yéle to Wyclef for his performance at the Monte Carlo event, organized by a for-profit company with a percentage of proceeds going to Yéle; the second was for the purchase by Yéle of discounted airtime and production for programming about Yéle themes and activities from a television company in Haiti owned by Wyclef and Jerry; the third involved the rental by Yéle of office space from the Platinum Sound recording studio in New York that is owned by Jerry.

Details of the above "big three" related-party transactions were reviewed by Yéle's accountants and lawyers, and came under scrutiny by an independent external auditor and later a forensic auditor. They all agreed that there was no misconduct on Yéle's part. However, this did not prevent the media from jumping to conclusions before checking on the details connected with the transactions.

The bulk of the money used to fund the programs of Yéle on the ground in Haiti for the five years from 2005 to 2009 did not go through the US chapter. That money came from Comcel/Voilà, the cell phone company—later the Voilà Foundation—and went directly into the bank account of the Haiti chapter of the organization. The latter was created in 2005 as a separate, stand-alone legal entity, registered as an

NGO under the laws of Haiti. I had overall responsibility for managing the funds that came into the Haiti account and for making sure that records and receipts were kept.

The US chapter of Yéle was responsible for raising money to send to the Haiti chapter, as well as generally helping to raise awareness of Yéle's work in specific, and the needs of Haiti in general. When management of the US chapter fell apart in the first half of 2006, I was asked to take it over. At that time, because I was running the operation in Haiti and overseeing all the programs, including the huge YéleFest in December of 2006, I did not really take this new assignment seriously until early in 2007.

It took until December 2009 to sort out the US chapter. At a meeting of the US board of Yéle in New York that month, I was able to report that external audits had been completed for each year from 2005 to 2008, that outstanding tax returns had been submitted to the IRS for those years and, happily, that the IRS had agreed that there would be no fines for late filing of those returns. At the same time, we had now formally adopted all the policies necessary for operating a non-profit in the United States.

I was hugely relieved to have the US chapter back on track. To this end, I called a meeting of the US board of directors in New York on January 12, 2010 to mark the start of an entirely new phase of Yéle Haiti. After much work by a large number of people over the course of several years, the past problems had all been addressed and everything was now in place for a smooth-functioning operation. The meeting was drawing to a close at 5:00 p.m. when our cell phones began to ring. Wyclef was the first to answer and he shared the news that there had just been an earthquake in Haiti.

3

ONWARDS FROM ARMAGEDDON:

*Providing Emergency Services to Earthquake
and Cholera Victims*

HAITI, 2010. On January 12, 2010, just before 5:00 p.m. local time, Haiti was hit by a massive 7.0 magnitude earthquake. Port-au-Prince was the worst hit, but the southern port city of Jacmel also sustained extensive damage. It is estimated that around 220,000 people died, including more than 16,000 government employees, and some 300,000 people were injured. Close to 4,000 schools were damaged or destroyed. In Port-au-Prince, the National Palace and the Parliament collapsed, as did 60 percent of all government and administrative buildings. The national Cathedral was in ruins. Before long, some 600,000 people had fled the capital to seek shelter in other parts of the country, while 1.5 million of those who stayed were soon living in makeshift tent camps because their homes had collapsed or were no longer inhabitable.

A similar earthquake in a country where building codes are enforced would have caused a fraction of the damage, but in Port-au-Prince, it took less than sixty seconds to create the largest urban disaster in sixty years. An estimated 671 million cubic feet of rubble and debris was created as buildings collapsed, enough to fill standard fifty-foot-long railway boxcars stretching from New York City to Dallas, Texas.

Within hours, we began to explore how to provide immediate assistance to the victims of the earthquake. But within days, we were also faced with a tidal wave of negative media coverage about the organization. I will begin with what we did to help victims.

Starting over

The day after the earthquake, Wyclef, Jerry and Claudinette, Wyclef's wife, flew to the Dominican Republic and made their way to Port-au-Prince by road because the airport in the capital was closed. They gathered together some of the Yéle team, and together helped pick up bodies from the streets. The truck they were using to take the bodies away was being driven by a young Yéle staffer named Jean Bernard Delsaint, who went by the nickname Fanfan. In his mid 20s, this young man was so dedicated that he had tattooed Wyclef's name on his arm. Fanfan was left with the truck loaded with bodies while Wyclef and the others set out on foot to find places to bury the corpses, and when they returned they found Fanfan dead. According to a passenger in the vehicle, who had escaped, Fanfan had been shot when a group of armed men tried to steal the truck and he refused to let them take it.

Wyclef and Jerry were back in New York within a week. Phones were not working in Haiti and so they had been out of touch. We learned only on their return that we had lost two members of the Yéle team: Fanfan had been murdered and Jean Jimmy Alexandre, known as Jimmy O, had died when a building fell on the car he was driving. Many of the team had lost family members, and more than half had lost their homes.

Jimmy O, as I have mentioned earlier, had been a vital part of Yéle since the very first, and had tirelessly used his position as a popular hip-hop musician to lead programs for us. He had been among the musicians who first went into barricaded Cité Soleil with rice in 2005, and was by my side when I went there later that year to negotiate with the notorious gang leader Amaral. Jimmy led a group of musicians who toured the country for almost two years performing songs they wrote about safe sex and preventing HIV/AIDS. He was only five and a half feet tall and thin as a rail, but with a fiery spirit that was contagious and a smile that could light up a room.

In order to make a meaningful contribution in the aftermath of the devastation, Yéle had to discontinue all the programs we had been managing and supporting and start again from scratch. The first priority was to provide direct assistance to the estimated 1.5 million people who were now living in tents and makeshift shelters.

As news of the earthquake spread, there was an outpouring of support from around the world. Many governments, led by the United States, sent in military and other teams specializing in disaster response. The public responded in record numbers by making donations to NGOs that were providing assistance, including Yéle. It is estimated that one out of every two American households donated to Haiti relief efforts. Many contributed using their cell phones, making this the first widespread utilization of text messaging to make donations in response to a humanitarian crisis. Individual volunteers, particularly in the medical field, began to arrive in Haiti. Many NGOs, including a number that had never been there before, began to send teams to help out. And emergency supplies began to arrive at the airport in Port-au-Prince.

Yéle's first coordinated effort was to collect and airlift food, medical supplies, blankets, and windup flashlights and radios. It was not until I arrived in Port-au-Prince on January 24th in connection with one of those airlifts that I understood how many other organizations and governments had the same idea. FedEx had donated a plane to Yéle that we shared with two other NGOs to transport supplies. That plane had landed earlier in the day and I arrived that afternoon in a military aircraft, as there were no passenger planes allowed at that time. The airport was a madhouse. The main terminal and the control tower had been damaged, and the airport only re-opened when the US military took it over and turned it into a military rather than a civilian operation. Planes were landing all day long filled with emergency supplies, but there was no system on the ground for receiving the material. The contents of each plane would be unloaded onto the runway and then it would take off.

Soon the US military designated a field next to the airport and all supplies were taken there as soon as they were dropped off. Most everything had been shipped on standard 4-by-4-foot wooden pallets, on which supplies had been secured by ropes, straps, mesh or plastic sheets. The resulting assemblies ranged from three to ten feet high, depending on the contents. Imagine two muddy football fields put together end to end, covered with thousands of pallets loaded with emergency supplies, food, mobile generators, building parts for temporary hospitals and clinics, tents packaged and ready to be assembled, and so on. This site became known informally as "the village," although technically it never existed because it was never officially sanctioned. But the supplies had to go somewhere other than the runway.

After landing, I walked to "the village" to try to locate the supplies that had come in on our FedEx flight a few hours earlier. There were US soldiers keeping order at the site, but they politely explained that they were not there to manage the pickup of supplies. In fact, there was no one to assist in this regard, and each NGO had to go around and look at the shipping number on pallets to try and find their own items. It took hours, but our pallets were finally located. I returned soon afterwards with some of the local Yéle team and the large truck we had previously used for food distributions. No one monitored who came and who left the area. No one asked to see our credentials or checked that we were leaving with only what belonged to us. The whole experience made it clear that, at the international level, some kind of force is needed that could be deployed in the days immediately following a natural disaster of this kind to provide basic coordination among all those offering assistance, not least those sending supplies. If the earthquake in Haiti is an accurate measure, none of the existing post-disaster units deployed from various parts of the world—however well-intentioned—is competent to manage something on this scale.

Nine members of the local Yéle team came with me to collect our materials, which consisted of nutrition bars, bottled water, boxes of basic medical supplies designated for one of the hospitals, new blankets and sheets in their wrapping, and battery-free flashlights and radios that were powered by cranking a handle. Because we had no forklift, we had to unwrap the pallets in order to load them onto the truck, transferring all the contents by hand. At one point I saw several members of the team taking some items and setting them aside, and, from a distance, it looked as if they were emergency materials. I had already handed

Yéle delivering hot meals, food, clothing, tents, blankets and other emergency supplies to tent camps following the January, 2010 earthquake.

Tanker trucks delivering fresh water to the tent camps. Author Hugh Locke is working the faucet on one of the trucks to fill buckets brought to collect the water.

Sebastian Petion.

Yéle Corps employed 2,000 people at a time from the tent camps to clean streets and collect garbage. In their distinctive blue uniform with the Yéle logo, they were a common sight around Port-au-Prince.

Sebastian Petion.

Another post-earthquake program commissioned smallholder farmer members of the Afe Neg Combite cooperative to grow fresh vegetables, supplied weekly to thirty-five orphanages to improve nutrition.

Sebastian Petion.

Working with Estime Lucienne, leader of the Place Fierte Soleil tent camp (11,000 residents) in the Port-au-Prince slum of Cité Soleil, shown here with author Hugh Locke. Behind me are colleagues Joe Mignon and Carlene Blanchfield.

Sebastian Petion.

Following the cholera outbreak in late 2010, Yéle deployed workers to tent camps to distribute soap and hand sanitizer, and conduct preventive hand-washing demonstrations.

Yéle's efficient supply chain bringing donated goods by plane and ship from the U.S. and Canada. Once in Haiti, the goods were stored at our headquarters (shown here) and then distributed to tent camps by our team.

A Yéle Corps vocational training program in carpentry, masonry, and plumbing (late 2010). The six-month intensive training was followed by assistance in securing jobs.

each of them a supply for their families, knowing they were all affected by the earthquake, and I immediately jumped to the conclusion that they were taking an additional amount. I approached and demanded to know what they were doing, expecting them to be embarrassed to be caught in the act. They were all silent for a minute, until one of them explained that they had folded up the plastic wrapping from the pallets that I had instructed be thrown out. They were taking the wrapping home because it was needed for temporary shelters and plastic of this kind was in short supply. I felt foolish, but it was a valuable reminder about the reality of the situation being faced by millions of people.

Yéle had just rented a house with more than an acre of walled, open space around it, in an area near the airport known as Santos. This was now our headquarters. The truck was unloaded into the house, and over the next few days the supplies were taken to various tent camps and distributed by the Yéle team.

Two weeks after the earthquake, this informal distribution had evolved into a major program to supply hot meals and clean drinking water to the tent camps. We had found a Haitian food company that was willing to purchase bulk food from sources in both the Dominican Republic and Haiti, and to prepare hot meals in a catering facility that had been only slightly damaged in the earthquake. With minimum repairs, this facility was soon able to produce an average of 6,500 meals at a time. Every few days over the next two months we would take these meals—in Styrofoam containers, each with a portion for two people consisting of rice, beans, and a stew of either chicken or meat—and distribute them in various tent camps. In the end we gave out a total of 98,000 hot meals. While the majority of those meals went to people in tent camps, we also provided some to members of the national police force who were themselves living in tents, as the government was unable to give them any food or wages for the first month and a half following the earthquake. We also provided meals during that same time for a number of civil servants who were in a similar situation, but who were determined to stay on the job to do what they could to restore services for the population.

I helped many times with the hot meal distribution. People were so grateful to get the food, and they were also grateful that we presented it to them with dignity. There were many instances during that time when food was being dropped from helicopters or thrown from the back of moving trucks as people ran to grab what they could. Yéle was one of the first NGOs to set up a well organized program, consulting in advance with the tent camp leaders to determine how many people were in the camp so that we brought enough food, and then arranging for residents of the camp to be involved in letting the residents know what to expect. The results were certainly not without incident, but it was generally orderly and did not involve the kind of riots that were being shown on television.

One particular distribution stands out in my mind. We had taken the Yéle truck, laden with hot meals, to a tent camp in Cité Soleil that went by the name of "Place Fierte Soleil," in reference to the public park on which it stood. My job that day was to make sure the line of around 600 people waiting to receive their hot meals remained orderly. As someone approached and tried to break into the line, I would intervene and make them go to the back. Each time I did this there would be voices of thanks from those waiting patiently in the blazing sun. I noticed a particularly frail elderly couple in the line. I approached them and, using my limited French and, more importantly, some hand gestures, I asked the crowd for permission to take this couple to the front of the line. There was a general murmur of consent as I escorted them to the truck where the meals were being handed out. It was not too long before a pregnant woman standing in the line signaled to me, and I got the same expression of consent from the crowd and took her to the front. When they requested it, I was able to help several more elderly people and pregnant women, each time approved by the crowd. People consented readily because the line was already moving along and they were making steady progress towards the source of the food. At that point, another pregnant woman approached. She had not been in the line up to that point, but I made the same entreaty to the crowd as before and was shocked when they all began to shout at once. It turned out that this local woman was not pregnant at all, but had stuck a pillow under her dress. She managed to fool me, but not her neighbors in the line who knew full well that she had shown no signs of pregnancy until that moment. I burst out laughing and the crowd gave me a hearty round of applause as I sent the woman to the back of the line.

We also had a program for providing clean drinking water. We were renting space for our headquarters from a commercial company that had a purification plant on the property and drew water from underground aquifers. We were able to contract with them to lease their fleet of fourteen 1,200-gallon tanker trucks to deliver close to 34,000 gallons a day to people in tent camps. Over the course of eleven months, we distributed nearly 4.2 million gallons of water. It was particularly gratifying to see people patiently lining up with containers to collect water from a faucet on each truck. In contrast with many of the scenes being shown on the news at that time, they were always calm and orderly. It was Jerry who had the vision for this water program and continued as its tireless champion.

During the first few months following the earthquake, Yéle was delivering emergency supplies, hot meals, and clean water to an average of sixteen tent camps a week. We estimated that we were reaching an average of 50,000 people on a regular basis one way or another. The US side of our team had expanded to include Joe Mignon, Carlene Blanchfield, and Karen Pardini. Lorena Gutierrez came on board to set up a base of operation in Miami for storing and shipping supplies, and to help with distributions in Haiti. Assisted by our existing team on the ground in Haiti, each was instrumental in helping my long time colleague, Suzie Sylvain, and me to oversee our various operations, We also had a range of volunteers in New York without whose help we would not have been able to cope.

Yéle was now a completely different organization from what it had been before the earthquake. We felt it appropriate to mark this transition by switching the colors of our logo from orange and black to red and blue, the colors of the Haitian flag. It was a small change to our image that reflected the significantly broader changes in our new scale of operation.

Media storm

The day after the earthquake we posted information on our website to let people know how they could make a US$5 text donation to Yéle using their cell phones. We had no idea how people would respond, but within a short time we were getting up to 5,000 donations an hour. As mentioned earlier, texting donations was a new phenomenon and the first time it caught on in response to a disaster. When people made a donation, they would let their friends know and many would follow a donation by talking about Yéle on social media sites. Soon we were receiving several hundred thousand dollars a day and getting calls from the media because of the volume of text donations coming in. This media interest was added to what was being generated by Wyclef as a Haitian celebrity and the fact that we were one of the only non-profit organizations devoted solely to Haiti.

On January 14, just two days after the earthquake, the first negative media story came out on a gossip website. As recounted in the previous chapter, Yéle had made payments in 2006 for services in support of our charitable mission that were provided by companies owned by Wyclef and Jerry. In addition, the article stated—erroneously—that we had failed to file with the IRS for the years 2005 to 2008, and the author neglected to mention that all four years had been submitted (admittedly late) and accepted by the IRS without any penalties, and that we had conducted external audits for all four of those years.

The original gossip website story was picked up by other websites and, within a few days, began to be covered by more serious outlets. Soon Yéle and Wyclef were being vilified by a broad spectrum of media, implying that our past missteps were proof that people should not trust us with donations for earthquake relief.

We decided to hold a press conference in New York on January 18th to tell our side of the story. It was attended by some eighty member of the press, including at least a dozen television stations. Wyclef spoke first of his work with Yéle and clarified that he had not profited personally from the organization. He became very emotional when describing how he had picked up dead bodies only a few days earlier. I followed and spoke at length about our programs in Haiti before the earthquake and what we were now preparing to do in the tent camps.

While most of the press conference coverage continued to focus only on the negative, I was grateful for a few stories that introduced some balance. A story on one of the CNN online sites was particularly encouraging when they said, "…tax experts say it's routine for individuals to charge their own charities, so long as services are being provided in return." They went on to quote Marcus Owen, former chief of the IRS unit that oversees non-profits, who said, "the tax rules do not prohibit related party transactions." Owen went on to say that Yéle's IRS filing for 2006 "also stated that the charges were 'below market'." This is an important distinction supporting legitimacy, according to Owen, who said that rules require that they be at no more than market value.

I learned two important media lessons from this experience: first, that even if you are found "not guilty" by the experts who know about the finer points of the law, the verdict can often linger as "guilty" in the court of public opinion; second, I observed that celebrities can be as effective at generating negative as positive press, even when they are completely silent. Just the fact that a celebrity is involved, in this case Wyclef, keeps the story going much longer than would otherwise be the case.

The press conference was followed by weeks of interviews. Almost daily, I had long discussions with reporters who were only interested in uncovering dirt on Wyclef and Yéle. Most were not even willing to feign interest in what we were actually doing on the ground to help earthquake victims. I finally stopped answering the phone and decided that the best counter to all the accusations was to get to work helping the victims in Haiti.

From behind bars

While the media coverage largely ignored the good work we were doing, we continued to receive support from a wide range of individuals, organizations, and businesses. I was particularly heartened by donations from prisoners in the United States. Until then, I did not realize that prisoners could make charitable donations. Then we began to receive US Treasury checks from the Bureau of Prisons. It turned out that individual prisoners were giving up their modest pay for work in the prisons and having the resulting checks sent to Yéle Haiti as a contribution towards earthquake relief. Most of the checks were for US$5 or US$10.

When they first began to arrive, we thought maybe an enthusiastic prisoner or guard in one prison had organized inmates to donate to Yéle. But before long we had received donations from a total of 141 prisoners in 23 different prisons, all in the form of checks issued by the Bureau of Prisons. It was a spontaneous and uncoordinated outpouring of support.

Dozens of these checks were accompanied by letters from prisoners, and in most they identified themselves as being either Haitian- or African-American. One inmate wrote, "You are a strong people with a rich heritage, being the first of us Africans in the diaspora to throw off the yoke of slavery in the western hemisphere. It is now time to unify and rise as a collective people to rebuild your lives and re-establish Haiti, and the Haitian people, on the international stage." He went on to say, "Once again you will be the model for others that are dealing with adverse situations of our own." In what could be an anthem for Haiti, he concluded, "I have faith in the human spirit to rise above disaster."

One particularly poignant letter was written in Braille and accompanied a US$5 check. Once we found someone to translate, the prisoner's message began, "To my brothers and sisters in Haiti, I know you are hurting now but things will get better." He ended his letter with, "Just know that we are praying every day for you guys out there."

Emergency relief

In the first two and a half months of our new post-earthquake mission, Yéle was successful in providing support to those in tent camps. At first, the emphasis had been on responding to emergency conditions. But things were settling down a bit from the initial chaos, and it was now time to consolidate our operation and take it to the next level of scale and efficiency. There were two aspects to this transformation: supplies and distribution.

The supplies related to donated items from the United States that were sent to Haiti by ship in forty-foot containers. Our initial flow of supplies had been by air, but that only made sense during the period immediately following the earthquake. Once the ports were reopened, it was more cost-effective to transport goods by ship. And the volume of what we were sending had increased greatly, as people began to see that we had the capacity to distribute emergency supplies efficiently to tent camps.

Some of that increase in materials was due to individual companies and organizations offering a wide range of items from T-shirts to packaged food to wheelchairs and even an ambulance. But at least half the increase was due to one person, Claudinette Jean, Wyclef's wife. She began volunteering shortly after the earthquake and soon proved to be a human dynamo as she put together a collection center in South Orange, New Jersey, where people could drop off items to be sent to Haiti. She assembled a local team, and together they reached out to community organizations, churches, schools, and businesses with a list of what was needed, including clothing, shoes, medical supplies, personal toiletries, and other items.

Following a disaster, people typically want to donate such items, but they are discouraged by the more established NGOs, who can only deal with bulk amounts of any given item. It is not cost-efficient for them to sort random items that people might want to donate, and they do not have a system in place at the disaster site for distributing anything other than bulk amounts of standardized items. A line from one charity website summed it up when they wrote, "Don't donate goods. Donating stuff instead of money is a serious problem in emergency relief." Claudinette designed a system that brilliantly addressed this issue by combining the sorting of the random items together with a system for delivering them in the tent camps. Everything that was dropped off at the South Orange center was immediately sorted into bags designed to be given to individuals in the camps. There were different colored bags for women, men, girls, boys, and pregnant or recent mothers. The bags were filled with new and used clothing, toiletries, food, and other items appropriate for each target group. The contents were never the same from batch to batch, but it always included a range of useful items. At the Haiti end, what we came to call "care bags" would be taken by the Yéle team into various tent camps and distributed. The different colored bags made it easier to manage the distributions in the often difficult circumstances in the tent camps.

As the supply of emergency relief items increased, we had to rent a warehouse in New Jersey in addition to the one we were already renting in Miami in order to have two staging areas for storage and for packing items onto pallets ready for shipping. When a container arrived at the port in Haiti, it was transferred to a truck and driven to our headquarters, where we built a large concrete platform on which we placed nine, permanent forty-foot containers. The contents of each container that arrived on site would then be transferred to one of the permanent containers. This was more cost effective than building a new warehouse, as there was no such facility on the property we were renting.

By April, we were sending an average of one forty-foot container a week to Haiti, a level which continued until the end of 2010.

For the first few months following the earthquake, the government of Haiti waived the normal customs procedures in order to get emergency supplies through in a timely manner. When that grace period was over, we prepared an internal document that detailed the seventeen separate steps the government was demanding for customs clearance. In this truly arcane and bureaucratic system, if you happened to be on Step 13 and the stamp you had just been given for Step 12 was updated, you had to start the entire process again. The only thing missing to complete this Dickensian dock scene were quill pens and parchment. The flow of our containers began to slow down, despite scrupulously following the seventeen steps. It then dawned on us that we were ignoring one crucial but unwritten step: offering bribes. After some delicate negotiations, we convinced the officials concerned that the bribe—set at US$300 per container—would be termed a "facilitation fee," and an invoice would be issued for each container so that it could be properly accounted for.

The significant increase on the supply side was matched by a greatly increased distribution system on the ground in Haiti. Yéle had always had its finger on the pulse of the local communities in the slums, and we drew on that capacity when designing our distribution system for tent camps. Two people were principally responsible: Joe Mignon had a background in social work in the U.S., spoke Creole, and was part of the New York team of Yéle. Ismick Beljour, known to all of us by his family name, was a longtime community activist who had been an invaluable part of the Yéle team since 2008. Together, they were able to find tent camps that were well organized and were not getting enough supplies from other NGOs or agencies.

It is important to note here that the tent camps were by no means all the same. There were literally hundreds of camps throughout Port-au-Prince and the surrounding area with an estimated 1.5 million inhabitants. For the most part, people were living in these camps because they had no other choice: either they had lost their homes, families had lost the wage earner who supported them, or their world was severely disrupted by the general collapse of the economy following the earthquake. However, there were also tent camps that were established in strategic locations to make a political statement. Some people who otherwise had a job and an income were living in tent camps in order to save rent money. Still others remained in their previous house or apartment, but set up a tent so that they would be eligible for handouts from NGOs, and would only show up at the camp when those supplies were about to be delivered. I am not explaining this to assign blame or express outrage. Life for the average citizen of Haiti has long involved unimaginable hardships, but at the same time we wanted to make sure that Yéle supplies were only going to the most deserving.

Yéle had expanded its operation and now served thirty-four tent camps on a regular basis. Together, they served 79,783 people. How did we come by such a precise number? We conducted our own survey by hiring local university students whose schools had collapsed or were damaged and sending them out with clipboards. This was part of taking our operation to the next level—we needed to know how many people were in each camp. How many separate tents or shelters were in each? What was the breakdown between men and women? How many children were there? How many were school age? What services were already being provided and by which NGOs or agencies, so we would not duplicate what was already being provided? The survey was completed in early May and was the most comprehensive and detailed assessment of tent camps to date, although it was limited to the thirty-four that we were serving at that time. That number shrank to thirty by the end of 2010, as some camps began to close.

Each tent camp had a different personality. Some were run like military operations. Others were very enterprising and had set up informal schools. In some camps everyone kept their tents neat and clean, inside and out, including potted plants and painted stones that delineated the equivalent of a front yard. However, the majority of sites were dirty from a combination of mud and garbage, although inside the tents were almost universally clean and well organized. Some camps coordinated cooking for all the residents, while in others each family was on their own. There were camps that organized regular soccer games for the youth, while others put on musical performances at night.

The camp that I was most directly involved with was called Place Fierte Soleil, in the Port-au-Prince slum of Cité Soleil. The reason for my involvement was the camp leader, Estime Lucienne. It was unusual for a camp leader to be a woman, especially for one with a population of 10,630 (according to our survey). Estime was in her early 40s, of medium height and build, and with very dark skin. Although living in a tent camp, she was always well turned out, consistently wearing jewelry that matched her outfits, although the quality of the accessories would not have made her a target for even the most desperate of criminals. But she was charismatic and outspoken, and had been a respected community leader before the earthquake, a mother of three, and a "mambo," or female priest, in the Vodou religion.

When I first met Estime, Beljour had already included the Place Fierte Soleil tent camp among those Yéle would serve. Within five minutes of our first meeting, she challenged me to do more for her camp. She was not aggressive or rude, simply forthright and direct. I knew they were not receiving much support from the other NGOs, not least because Cité Soleil is such a dangerous place to work. I both liked and trusted Estime, and we were soon deep in discussion about precisely what they needed. We started by clearing away one section of the camp that had the most dilapidated shelters. Because one of the main complaints was that the entire area turned into a mud pit when it rained, a simple system of drainage was installed and a layer of gravel added. Then we installed several hundred tents. Another NGO had previously installed some toilets for the camp, but in the absence of a proper sewage system, the toilets were useless, not to mention pungent. So we installed two large underground septic tanks and built twelve new toilets and, for the first time in the camp, twelve showers. None of this would have been possible without the exceptional skills of a builder and contractor named Warnel Pierre. Assisted by Joe Mignon and Carlene Blanchfield, Warnel was able to work under the most arduous circumstances and accomplish outstanding results. His supplies would be stolen, he and his workers often threatened by thugs in the area, and he frequently had trouble convincing equipment rental companies that their cranes, backhoes, or other items would not disappear overnight. But he persevered and the results were excellent.

I readily admit favoritism in the case of Place Fierte Soleil. They definitely got more than any of the other tent camps. At one point I arranged for Cirque d'Haiti, a clown and acrobat troupe supported by Cirque du Soleil, to come and perform for around 600 children at the camp. They were absolutely mesmerized and, for an hour or so, they were able to just be themselves and not kids stuck in a tent camp. As the performance ended, we had arranged for a local *rara* band to lead a procession through the camp. Every neighborhood in the poor sections of Port-au-Prince has its own *rara* band. While its origins are connected to Vodou, these bands now perform in street processions that mark special events of all kinds and are particularly in evidence during the annual pre-Lenten Carnival and during Easter week. Their instruments are usually made by hand, often from recycled metal, and include a range of horns, drums, bells and an assortment of what can only be described as noise makers. Singers are included in this mix, and their lyrics are often either directly political or, at the very least, address issues such as poverty and oppression. It is hard to imagine a more exuberant and uninhibited form of musical expression than hundreds of children being led by a *rara* band in a procession through a tent camp in Cité Soleil. If the acrobats and clowns were magical, this experience was transporting… and extremely noisy.

By April following the earthquake, a bird's eye view of Yéle headquarters on a typical weekday would show fourteen large tanker trucks filled with clean water leaving the compound in the morning and returning around noon, when they would get refilled and then go out again for an afternoon delivery. In addition to this fleet, Yéle trucks would come and go several times a day, making various deliveries to tent camps. When these trucks were accompanied by a minivan, it often meant the truck would be carrying tents and the Yéle team in the van would be helping to set up the tents when they arrived at a camp. When our flatbed truck went out, it was usually carrying pouches of water: Haitians in poor communities are used to drinking water from 10-ounce plastic pouches, so we produced these for free distribution, in addition to delivering water in tanker trucks. By the end of 2010, we had tracked the delivery of close to 4.2 million gallons of filtered water in tanker trucks; 294,000 pouches of water; 2,120 tents of various sizes, 14,300 pounds of medical supplies, 3,740 windup radios and flashlights; just over 5,000 care bags; 270,310 nutrition bars; and 3,520 pairs of new and used shoes. This is by no means a complete list, but it gives a sense of the operation. And every delivery was documented by a form attached to a clipboard that described the items in detail, signed and verified by our staff when it left the Yéle compound, and then countersigned upon arrival by the tent camp leader and a witness from the camp, both of whom counted the items coming off the truck. Having both the camp leader and a witness was important so that the residents had a way to monitor what was coming in from Yéle and the camp leader could not be accused of withholding supplies from the community.

During this period we also gave a substantial grant to a medical NGO called Project Medishare for the purchase the first high resolution CT scanner to be available to patients in Haiti regardless of their financial resources. Project Medishare operated the only trauma and critical care hospital in Haiti at that time. But this being Haiti, when the scanner finally arrived, there was a problem. The scanner was a very complicated piece of equipment housed in a forty-five-foot trailer that could not be subjected to any big bumps while en route to the hospital. The roads along the way were anything but ideal for this purpose, as they were replete with crater-sized potholes. In the end, we had gravel trucks and volunteers at strategic points so that, as the scanner approached, the uneven spots and potholes could be filled. Although it took a year to finally get the scanner to Haiti following the earthquake, it was rewarding to know that at least those seeking follow-up care from their injuries could be treated more effectively.

One of my other favorite post-earthquake programs involved orphans and farmers. We received a grant from the Hard Rock Café chain of restaurants as part of their involvement with an NGO called Why Hunger. Their generous contribution allowed Yéle to contract a 6,000 member farmers' cooperative, known as Afe Neg Combite led by a charismatic Catholic priest, Father Cico, to grow vegetables that supplemented the diet of children in orphanages. Every Saturday we delivered baskets with 150 to 200 pounds of fresh vegetables to thirty-five orphanages that between them were home to around 2,000 children. The whole operation was designed and managed for Yéle by a particularly competent young Haitian American named Samuel Darguin, who later went on to found an innovative NGO called the Haitian American Caucus.

Jobs and job training

While water, food, tents, and emergency supplies were very important, an equally important issue was jobs. People in the tent camps were desperate to start earning a living again. Our response was to create an employment program with a job training component.

Before describing this initiative, a comment is needed about unemployment statistics. The most recent published estimate indicates that

40.6 percent of the labor force in Haiti is out of work, ranking it 187 out of 200 countries for unemployment. But this statistic does not reflect the informal economy of Haiti accurately. Few people in the country have the kind of salaried jobs that are traditionally considered when compiling these rankings. But everywhere you go in Haiti, people are engaged in commerce. Sometimes their entire inventory will consist of ten oranges artfully arranged on a square of cloth on the street. Or it might be a dozen electronic gadgets balanced on a vendor's head while going from car to car in busy traffic. My personal favorite is the daily emergence of temporary outdoor art galleries with paintings and metal sculptures mounted on walls throughout Port-au-Prince. Such enterprises may not count as formal jobs with a paycheck, but it is evidence of people's impulse to earn a living by whatever means they can. When this informal economy is not taken into consideration in official employment statistics, you don't get an accurate economic profile of the country. Nor is there an accurate representation of people's willingness to work.

As had always been the case with Yéle programs, the impetus for our employment initiative came from Wyclef and I then put the pieces in place. We decided to replicate Pwojè Lari Pwòp, the street-cleaning operation that Yéle had been part of from 2005 to 2007. It had been managed by the Pan American Development Foundation, with Yéle as the brand and responsible for community relations, but this time around we decided to run the whole thing ourselves. The concept was the same: hire people from poor communities to collect garbage and clean the streets. The difference this time was that the workers came from the tent camps.

Yéle Corps, as we called it, was the single largest program we had ever attempted on our own up to this point. We would not have progressed past the idea stage had it not been for Samuel Louis. He had been part of the management of the original Pwojè Lari Pwòp and agreed to head our new program. As Samuel and I began to prepare the plans, I was reminded again just how challenging it is to work in Haiti. It is one thing to employ people and supervise them collecting garbage, but then what do you do with the garbage? The civil authorities have never played more than a token role in garbage removal, so we had to create the entire operation ourselves. The original plan was to employ 1,000 people at a time and, after consulting experts in this field, we calculated that the collection would generate 450 cubic meters a day that would have to be hauled to the municipal waste site. This translates to the monthly equivalent of 166 40-foot containers, which in turn entails a staggering cost for renting the trucks to haul that volume of garbage. And as if that were not enough of a challenge, we were obliged to pay an entrance fee at the municipal waste site, because the government does not provide enough money to operate the facility.

While Samuel was key to the management of Yéle Corps, it would never have been possible without a sizeable grant from the Hope for Haiti Now Telethon that had been organized by George Clooney following the earthquake, plus additional support from BET's SOS Saving OurSelves telethon. We began with a pilot operation in my favorite tent camp, Place Fierte Soleil. Twenty workers from there were hired and paid US$7 a day, well above the national average and higher than the official minimum daily wage of US$5. By August, we had 650 workers, and by the end of September we were employing 2,000 people in Yéle Corps, all receiving US$7 a day. This amounted to twice the originally projected number of workers, which also meant twice the volume of garbage to haul away, with each truck paying an entrance fee per visit to the municipal waste site.

Yéle Corps workers—wearing their distinctive uniform: a blue T-shirt and matching blue cap, with the Yéle logo on each—became a familiar site throughout Port-au-Prince. With a contingent of 2,000 they were hard to miss. The majority of the workers were drawn from the thirty-four tent camps we were supporting, and we always tried to ensure that roughly 20 percent were members of *rara* bands, given their important role in each community's informal political structure and in ensuring good community relations for the program.

At the first training session for team leaders and supervisors I met Anita André. She was living with her husband, three children and her mother in a tent camp, their home having been destroyed in the earth-quake. Samuel had singled her out from early interviews as being a poten-tial leader. The training session involved close to thirty people in total, but Anita was the only one who introduced herself after I had addressed the group. In equal measure, she was clearly leadership material and very proud to be in this job. She wore large gold hoop earrings, her signature look in coming months, even when in a Yéle Corps uniform, wearing boots, and directing workers with wheelbarrows full of garbage.

One day I asked Anita if I could visit her tent and meet her family. She was living in a tent camp directly in front of a restaurant where I con-ducted many business meetings at that time, and the irony was not lost, as I thought about sipping cappuccinos so close to Anita's meager abode. Her tent was not actually a tent: several posts held up tarps that formed the roof and sides of the structure. There were two rooms. The first had a small table and two chairs, and when a canvas flap was pulled aside you came to a second room that was completely taken up by a large mattress. All six members of the family slept together in this one bed. The place was immaculately clean—but not because she knew I was coming, as we had gone to the tent camp within minutes of my request to visit. All of their possessions were neatly stacked along one side of the first room. The only decoration I noticed was a shard from a broken mirror which had been carefully strung up and prominently displayed. I asked about cooking and was taken outside to where Anita's mother was preparing a midday meal on a charcoal grill. It was then that Anita turned to me and thanked me for her job. She explained that it meant her whole family now got one hot meal a day with the money she earned, whereas before, they had been existing on handouts, as neither she nor her husband had been able to find work since moving to the camp.

There were several "cash-for-work" programs like ours running at this time. While I commend any NGO that made the effort to provide employment, it always irritated me to see some of their workers stand-ing around doing nothing. There would often be a dozen people assigned to what was clearly a job for two, or entire teams of workers doing nothing while they waited for instructions. Samuel was both a brilliant organizer and a strict taskmaster, and he made sure that Yéle Corps workers were, to the degree possible, always fully engaged in purposeful tasks. This was not only for the sake of our reputation, but it was important to us that workers felt respected enough to be given a real job. There was such a long waiting list of people wanting to work for us that we only hired workers for four weeks at a time, and then took on a new contingent, except for the supervisors like Anita. And within the first few days of each new group coming onboard, we always fired a handful of people. This might seem harsh, given that they came from tent camps, but we had to maintain high standards and show that there were consequences for not taking the job seriously.

I will always remember one episode in the high-end business district of Port-au-Prince known as Petion-Ville. Here one block taken up with a tent camp and the next with stores where, despite the circumstances following the earthquake, you could still buy Christofle sterling silver flatware and Baccarat champagne flutes. I happened to be on the street in this area with Anita and her team of workers when a woman came storming out of a store and began screaming at the workers because she did not want them in front of her establishment. The women had not seen me until I walked over and positioned myself within inches of her well manicured face. I am afraid that all protocol training and manners were set aside as I let loose with expletives that are not in my daily lexicon. This entitled woman was undoubtedly happy to have the streets cleaned, but she did not want to get too close to those whom she perceived to be from a lower class. I stood with my arms crossed and refused to move, despite her protestations. She stomped back into her store to the sound of jubilant applause and shouts from the workers.

Another round of applause that will always stay with me took place on January 12, 2011. All 2,000 Yéle Corps workers were gathered together to mark the first anniversary of the earthquake. Wyclef was addressing them and asked for a minute of silence. This is not something that could normally be pulled off in Haiti, but the solemn nature of the day meant that you could have heard a pin drop. As it ended, people began to applaud. Sporadically at first, but more and more joined in. Before long it became a tumultuous roar of shouting and clapping that seemed to draw from some deep spiritual reservoir to erupt as an expression of hope and possibility.

Temporary employment programs like Yéle Corps made sense following the earthquake, but they are not long term solutions. To that end my colleagues Joe, Carlene, and Beljour created the vocational training component of Yéle Corps. In December of 2010, they launched a program that provided job training in the construction field for 112 youth and young adults, who received six months of vocational training in one of three fields: carpentry, masonry, and plumbing. They also got instruction in basic financial literacy, and at the end of the course were helped to find jobs.

Money, power, and housing

The broad political structure in Haiti prior to the earthquake continued afterwards. As mentioned earlier, the real power, funding, and decision making rests with a shadow government made up of foreign donor governments, international institutions, the United Nations and NGOs that together govern the country, quite separate and apart from Haiti's elected government. The main difference after the earthquake was that the number of international NGOs operating in the country more than tripled to as many as 10,000. The final tally will never be known, because there was no one to keep count. But Haiti began to be called the "republic of NGOs," based on the oft-repeated claim that the country had the highest number of foreign aid groups per capita in the world.

Since the 2010 earthquake, close to US$9 billion has been raised through public and private donations from around the world and spent on humanitarian and long-term relief aid in Haiti: this is money spent as of May, 2012 and does not refer to money that was pledged, but which has not yet been received or spent. The public money (roughly US$6 million) came from governments such as the United States, Canada, and Venezuela, as well as from institutions, like the World Bank and the International Monetary Fund. The private donations (estimated at US$3 billion) were made by the public (along with some foundations and corporations) to various charitable organizations.

The US$3 billion in charitable donations was either disbursed by the recipient organizations themselves, or given to other charitable organizations to use. Yéle received and disbursed close to US$14 million in response to the earthquake: US$8.7 million of that total was spent in 2010, the last year for which I was responsible, with 12.5 percent to cover overhead and administration.

The US$6 billion in public money from governments and international financial institutions was given mostly to international NGOs and private contractors, and only a fraction went to the Government of Haiti. Private contractors are commercial companies that specialize in building and implementing large scale infrastructure projects in developing countries. They do many of the same things that non-profits do, except that their bottom line is commercial rather than social.

The biggest public donor to Haiti was the US Government. As of May, 2012, they had disbursed close to US$2 billion, most of it to NGOs and contractors based in the United States. To be accurate, it is necessary to break down the US contribution into two categories: humanitarian (for immediate emergency needs following the earthquake) and rebuilding (longer term reconstruction and recovery). Out of US humanitarian funding, the Government of Haiti received zero, and out of the rebuilding funds they received 1 percent.

My source for much of this information is the excellent and exhaustively researched report "Haiti: Where Has All the Money Gone?" by Vijaya Ramachandran and Julie Walz, published by the Center for Global Development.

International NGOs and non-Haitian private contractors were functioning long before the earthquake, but afterwards, they had vast amounts of money and unquestionably ruled the day. That is not to say that this rule was smooth. In fact it was, and continues to be, a free-for-all in which the international NGOs and contractors are each doing their own thing without an overall plan or any attempt at coordination. The Government of Haiti is a minor bit player, while the UN uses its role as head of the peacekeeping troops as leverage to insert itself, without having any money to speak of, as the de facto policy setters and planners for the country in place of the national government.

The UN role was most evident when they convened "cluster" groups, following the earthquake, in order to gather together the international NGOs involved in various fields such as sanitation, food, water, housing, and so on. Haitian NGOs and Haitian government agency representatives were largely excluded from cluster meetings, and when they did attend, they tended to be ignored. To be fair, these meetings were occasionally useful, but for the most part, the UN used them to try to impose some sort of coordination among NGOs that already had their own agenda and funding, and who were often present to ensure that their territory was not encroached upon. Yéle took part in the early meetings, but I soon issued a ban on participation in the cluster system because it was fundamentally flawed.

Although the Government of Haiti lacks experience and is riddled with corruption, there comes a point when the international community must help them build the capacity to govern. Throughout their history, the contry's administration has been sidelined through the intervention of outsiders or highjacked by domestic dictators like the Duvaliers, who were, in turn, aided and abetted by outsiders. And there is always a reason to put off helping the government to improve. The time is never right. There is a hurricane, a food crisis, an earthquake, a cholera outbreak. During my time with Yéle, I saw firsthand the bedlam that can result from having no government in charge. International NGOs provided basic services in key areas, such as health and education, while foreign private contractors built infrastructure. But none of them work towards implementing a comprehensive, long-term plan for rebuilding the country. That plan does not exist because it could only come from a well functioning government. And the outsiders in a position to help transorm the government are not about to give up the funds and the power they already control. The result is barely orchestrated chaos.

There is probably no better example of this chaos than the situation of housing following the earthquake. I knew something was beginning to happen when I started getting calls from a bewildering array of companies from around the world wanting Yéle to assist them in gaining a foothold in Haiti in order to build temporary houses. After talking with the first three or four company representatives, I prepared a set of questions that I forced upon future callers, the first being: "Is your temporary housing system based on a proprietary panel system?" Most answered yes, and therein lay the main problem. Instead of using local labor to build houses, companies wanted to use prefabricated wall panels made with varying combinations of cement, metal, plastic, and insulation. Each had one or another variation of these combined materials, and each was able to get patents for what amounted to fundamentally the same panel. Moving some metal clips or changing the thickness of a layer of wire mesh allowed them to claim that it was unique and warranted a patent.

Next I asked, "Will all houses built using your panel system, now and in the future, require a royalty to be paid to an offshore, non-Haitian commercial entity?" By the time they heard this question, they were usually a little nervous, because the answer was invariably "yes." When I then asked, "Are you willing to show your commitment to the rebuilding of Haiti by building a factory there to produce these panels?" several seemed to see a glimmer of hope and were enthusiastic in responding with another "yes." But this was really just a setup, because my final question was, "Are you willing to build the factory without having a guaranteed order for the panels, and are you willing to confirm in writing that half of all profits will remain in Haiti." They usually hung up at that point.

Under the banner of humanitarian service, more than a hundred commercial companies came to Haiti with plans to build houses, both temporary and permanent, using some kind of proprietary system. Most involved prefabricated panels. Within this group there were certainly individuals who were motivated by a sincere desire to help, but the real challenge should be how to engage Haitians to rebuild and not to create dependence on imported prefabricated systems.

A few months after the earthquake, the Government of Haiti tried to get into the housing act. They issued a map titled "Government of Haiti – Housing Relocation Sites" showing three large plots of land in the vicinity of Port-au-Prince where NGOs could build houses for people in the tent camps. The explanation was that the government would invoke eminent domain, with the aim of forcing private land owners in these areas to sell their property for emergency housing. The government planned to purchase the land at fair market value and then turn it over at no charge to NGOs, on the condition that the NGOs paid for the resulting housing.

Yéle took this at face value—an unfortunate mistake on our part. I put together a team that included a builder, an engineer, and an agronomist. We conducted a survey of the three areas and settled on a 750-acre site perfectly suited to creating a new agricultural community. Our plan was to integrate advances in education, health, self governance, and micro-enterprise in building a new community for around 5,000 people that would be surrounded by farmland, on which we would implement agroforestry techniques to combine tree planting with increased food crop output. We did extensive planning, including a full layout of the housing, roads, services, and schools. We prepared a detailed proposal that showed the exact GPS coordinates of the 750 acres at the end of one of the three government-designated sites, near the Port-au-Prince suburb of Croix-des-Bouquets. I took Wyclef out to see the place and we walked through fields of corn and sorghum, with Wyclef getting excited about the possibilities of building a community there. The farmers we came across were rather confused seeing him on their land, but clearly excited by his presence. We felt it best not to explain that the government was about to expropriate their farms.

I then arranged for Wyclef and myself to meet with the cabinet member responsible for this operation. I am not mentioning him by name because I do not feel he was solely responsible for what happened. After presenting what I felt was a very comprehensive plan, complete with all the drawings and details of our agricultural community, the cabinet member professed to being very happy for us to proceed and told us to expect full government approval within two weeks. I asked about the next step and he said, "You need to figure out who owns the land." When I protested that this was surely the government's responsibility—particularly if they already had the mechanism in place to use eminent domain to acquire the land—he said, "We have no way of getting that information." Granted land ownership in Haiti is a complicated business that relies on laws that are a holdover from French colonial times, but this did not make sense.

The whole thing turned out to be a classic example of the government attempting a grand gesture which no one had thought through. Doubtless, there were politicians and civil servants who labored over various aspects of the scheme, but it seems they never all met in the same room to coordinate their efforts. It would have been comical, if it were not so sad. In the end, it became clear that the government had no capacity to implement this plan. They had created the map in a desperate attempt to appear to have a role in providing housing, but it was all conjecture. No land in any of the three locations set out on the original government-issued map was ever purchased by the government for use in building houses for earthquake victims.

The only tangible legacy of the government's housing plan is that today, as you drive north from Port-au-Prince along the coastal highway, Route Nationale, you will see thousands of tents and tarp structures. People from Port-au-Prince came to this desolate site when they heard that it was one of the three locations where the government was promising to build homes. Unlike the lush farmland we looked at, this is completely barren land with not a tree or bush in sight, and now dotted for many miles by thousands of temporary structures in which people are patiently waiting.

It is estimated that 105,000 houses were completely destroyed in the earthquake and another 188,383 badly damaged. So far US$9 billion has poured into Haiti to help the country recover from this disaster. This has resulted in approximately 120,000 one-room temporary shelters being built; however, fewer than 6,000 new permanent houses have been constructed and only some 15,000 damaged homes have been repaired using this money. Today, there are still some 200,000 people living in four major tent camps. It is all very well to point to the corruption of the government of Haiti, but is there not something fundamentally wrong when this much foreign aid is administered completely independent of the government and has so little impact? And of course there are additional complexities to be factored in, not least of which a land tenure system that seems sprung from the Middle Ages.

Were it not for foreign NGOs, most of the humanitarian assistance following the earthquake—and the majority of the ongoing social services at present—would not be provided. Theirs is a noble and needed service. But at what cost? If those services create a dependency and ultimately undermine the ability of an entire nation to function as a democracy, is that a price worth paying?

While this is indeed a bleak picture, there is one NGO that has been able to deliver basic services while at the same helping to build the capacity of the government. Partners in Health, which translates to Zanmi Lasante in Creole, introduced a community-based model of healthcare in 1985 and now operates throughout the country. They launched the world's first program to provide free, comprehensive HIV care and treatment in an impoverished setting, and are now a global model for the delivery of health care for complex diseases in community settings. And it is all done with the Ministry of Health as an active implementing partner, despite the fact that this involves providing training and support for the medical and administrative staff employed by the Ministry in its healthcare facilities in the field.

Trial by media

On August 4, 2010 Wyclef resigned from the board of Yéle and announced that he was going to run for president of Haiti. Minutes later, the phones in the Yéle office starting ringing and did not stop for months. The media storm we went through following the earthquake was not nearly as challenging as the one that followed this announcement. It continued long after Wyclef was officially disqualified on August 20, by which time it had been determined that he did not meet the residency requirements for presidential candidates, as set out in the constitution of Haiti.

Yéle provided the foundation for the press attack through the mistakes we had made in the past, as discussed previously, even though we had addressed those mistakes in as straightforward and transparent a manner as possible. We were able to show that these were errors in procedure and not anything more egregious. External auditors and the various experts we consulted at the time agreed with this assessment and helped set in place new procedures to ensure a smoother running operation that would avoid similar mistakes in the future. What we did not count on was that past mistakes, when combined with a celebrity running for public office, is a lethal and irresistible combination, because the mistakes then become the story. We had a responsibility, as a charitable organization, to explain and account for past errors. But in the face of an avalanche of invented stories that became a self-feeding and unchecked media phenomenon, we never got the chance to tell the whole story.

If politics can be a dirty business at times, the press is a willing and enthusiastic accomplice. And if you do not have the resources to engage in hand-to-hand combat with the media, you will be buried alive. Whether you are right or wrong is inconsequential; it is about having enough cash—for lawyers, publicists, media strategists and the other professionals who inhabit this space—to be able to stay in the fight and be heard above the noise of negative coverage. I naively thought that the truth would be enough to counter inaccurate and at times slanderous stories about Yéle, but I was completely wrong.

It was as if somewhere there was a "celebrity meter" that had signaled to the press that Wyclef, and by extension Yéle, was fair game and no outlet would call another on anything they invented in the course of trashing him and the organization. Instead, the unspoken agreement was that they would all repeat phrases and allegations from each other, regardless of how bizarre, outrageous, or untruthful they were. Three examples will help to illustrate the phenomenon.

On August 16, 2010, it was stated in an article in *The New York Times* by journalists Deborah Sontag and Stephanie Strom, entitled "Star's Candidacy in Haiti Puts Scrutiny on Charity," that "In early July,

Mr. Jean held a traffic-stopping rally to kick off a job creation program called Yéle Corps. Yéle paid 200 people US$7 each to surround him at the event and to pick up some garbage afterward. Then the workers were dismissed because the program had not yet been fully planned."

I met with Deborah Sontag in Haiti on August 7 and took her to see various Yéle programs, including a training session for Yéle Corps team leaders, inspectors and controllers. She was given copies of all the instruction materials, reporting forms and signup sheets that were part of that session, and had the opportunity to question everyone present, most of whom had been hired from tent camps. She asked me about the July event. I explained that the 200 people in question had been signed up to be among the first contingent of workers when the program was officially scheduled to begin on August 9. But because the July event was a few weeks in advance of that start date, we had felt it only proper to pay these workers for taking part in the event. I showed Deborah a list of all 200 workers in question and invited her to meet them when they began work the following Monday, August 9, so she could confirm that they had not been picked at random for a one day event and then forgotten. I introduced her to the Yéle staff member who had signed up each of the 200 workers, so that anything that was not clear about what they had been told could be explained. I introduced her to the Yéle Corps program director, Samuel Louis, and various senior team members, so she could get further verification, including that the standard day rate for the Yéle Corps program had long ago been set at US$7 and was not a random number chosen only for the event in July. Deborah did not show up on Monday to meet the workers in question and see the Yéle Corps program in operation, and the *Times* declined my request to print a correction regarding this and several other factual errors in the article.

The second example involves CNN. On August 6, 2010 Wolf Blitzer was interviewing Wyclef about his decision to run for president. Also on the show was Sean Penn, who gave a long explanation for why Wyclef should not run for president, saying, "I have not seen or heard anything of him in these last six months that I have been in Haiti… for those of us in Haiti, he has been a non presence."

While I admire Sean for his work in supporting a tent camp, I was puzzled by his statement. It seemed odd that he would say he was unaware of Wyclef, and by extension Yéle, when his J/P Haitian Relief Organization had been in direct discussions with Yéle four months earlier in an effort to get us to provide them with financial assistance. The executive director of the organization had met with one of Yéle's board members and, after reviewing our activities, had subsequently approached me. In an e-mail, the Executive Director said that J/P Haitian Relief was "working towards connecting Sean and Wyclef in the next month." I eventually turned down their request for money, explaining that we had a very full slate of our own programs to fund. The anticipated meeting with Wyclef did not take place. While Sean could not be expected to know everything that was being done in the name of his organization, surely this appeal to Wyclef and Yéle for funding would have been on his radar.

The following month Yéle received a request for water from some residents in Sean's tent camp. In response, we sent our tanker trucks on several occasions to provide clean water. We did not mention it to anyone, because we felt it was important to provide the service regardless of any political considerations.

The third example is more recent and involves Rupert Murdoch's *New York Post* and a November 27, 2011 article "Questions Dog Wyclef's Haiti Fund." Journalists Isabel Vincent and Melissa Klein wrote, "A purported Miami business called Amisphere Farm Labor Inc. received a whopping US\$1,008,000 as a 'food distributor.' No trace of the company could be found last week in the Sunshine State, but records show the company's head, Amsterly Pierre, bought three properties in Florida last year, including a condo in an upscale waterfront community."

The facts tell a quite different story: getting hot meals to people in tent camps was a priority immediately following the earthquake because they had limited capacity to cook in the camps. With this in mind we approached a businessman in Haiti with experience in this field, Amsterly Pierre, and asked him to set up the operation on our behalf. For this purpose, he used the bank account of a dormant but legally registered company he had in the U.S., Amisphere, because the banks were not yet functioning in Haiti. And because the payments were going from Yéle to Amisphere, the contractual relationship had to be between Yéle and Amisphere in order for us to wire the funds.

In the midst of the chaos that characterized Port-au-Prince at that time, Amsterly used his operation on the ground to find a kitchen that had sustained minimum damage in the earthquake and paid to have it repaired. He identified sources of food in both Haiti and the Dominican Republic, and assembled a local staff that could cook and deliver thousands of meals at a time.

The hot meal program began on January 24 with the first distribution of hot meals to tent camps. Over the next two months a total of 98,000 hot meals were served in the course of fifteen distributions with an average of 6,500 meals per distribution. Every distribution was fully documented, and payments to Amisphere were made periodically based on invoices that were checked against our distribution records.

In addition to the hot meals, we also contracted with Amsterly to develop a dry food ration kit. These were prepared in the Dominican Republic, brought to Haiti, and distributed in tent camps. Each kit had enough rations for an average family for one week. A total of 700 of these kits were distributed.

Yéle paid Amsterly US$10 per hot meal, which included transporting the meals to the tent camps where our staff distributed them. Each meal fed an average of two people, and the ration kits were estimated to feed five people for a week. Through Amsterly, Yéle was able to feed around 200,000 people at a cost of about US$5 per person, and this at a time when food was scarce, hot meals almost unheard of, and delivery of food into the tent camps regularly caused riots. The implication in the *Post* article was that we handed Amsterly money to buy a condo. They refused to publish a correction and were not interested in seeing any of the backup documentation related to the contract Yéle had with Amsterly and his company.

These three articles represented a larger pattern. *The New York Times* never wrote about Yéle employing 2,000 tent camp residents to clean the streets of Port-au-Prince, although many outlets picked up on the allegation that we faked a one-day cleanup operation. Sean Penn never acknowledged that his organization knew enough about Yéle to ask us for money, but his suggestion that Wyclef had done nothing to help Haiti following the earthquake was the focus of media coverage for months to follow. The *New York Post* never wrote about one of the most successful hot meal programs in the immediate aftermath of the earthquake, although their allegation that earthquake relief donations were used to buy a condo was repeated around the world.

Aside from an overwhelming sense of unfairness, the intensity of this media experience kept prompting me to understand it better. What took shape in my mind was a three-part explanation. We are all familiar with the emergence of the 24-hour news cycle and its relentless need for content, as well as the overall reduction in resources available for journalists to gather the news. This results in less original news gathering and a vast increase in the repetition of unsubstantiated stories from secondary sources. But a third factor added to this mix seems to be a reliance on archetypes as a substitute for good journalism. Wyclef is the proverbial "bad boy" who can do no good, according to the media, despite evidence to the contrary. And until he has been anointed in the press as having atoned for his perceived sins, we will continue to be fed negative stories. By contrast, Sean Penn, once the bad boy of Hollywood, but declared by the media as having redeemed himself through his actions, has been elevated to a sainthood that allows for no dissenting voices. These and other archetypes form a pantheon, once relegated to Jungian psychology, but now updated and applied exclusively to celebrities and public figures.

Cholera strikes

In October 2010, only nine months after the massive earthquake, Haiti was hit with yet another humanitarian crisis: a massive outbreak of cholera swept through the country. It started with UN peacekeepers from Nepal, who were stationed near the small town of Mirebalais, sixty miles north of Port-au-Prince, in an area called the Artibonite Valley. These soldiers were unwitting carriers of a virulent strain of cholera, but were themselves not sick with the disease. Human waste from outhouses at their UN base emptied directly into the country's largest river system without going through any sanitation facility, thereby introducing the cholera bacterium. The water-borne disease soon spread to Port-au-Prince and other parts of Haiti, and before long was labeled a full scale epidemic that continues to the present. As of April, 2012, the Centers for Disease Control and Prevention in Atlanta reported a total 534,647 cases of cholera since the outbreak began, 7,091 resulting in death.

When the epidemic began, there had been no recorded instances of cholera in Haiti for more than a century. It caught everyone off guard. The first thing I did upon hearing the news was to do a Google search to learn about symptoms and treatment. The second was to call Paul Farmer, one of the founding directors of Partners In Health, who was also serving as the UN's Deputy Special Envoy to Haiti. I asked what Yéle could do to help and explained that we had a program for delivering clean water to the tent camps. Within hours, we had set up an operation with Partners In Health (PIH), whereby they would send us a list of locations in the Artibonite Valley where our water tankers would go to be met by a PIH representative or other health practitioner and directed to places where the water was most needed. We started on October 23, the day after that phone call, and for a month and a half, Yéle delivered 17,000 gallons of water a day using this system, reducing it by half for an additional month.

The Yéle team that accompanied the first water trucks was frightened, as was the whole country. Rumors were spreading that the disease was air borne. This was not accurate, but people were panicking. To their credit, the Yéle team donned face masks and rubber gloves and did not hesitate to go into the infected area. The first convoy was delayed by a few hours, because it was reported on the radio that the main highway leading north from Port-au-Prince had been closed by the government in order to quarantine the outbreak. Other reports indicated that only vehicles with an official government *laissez-passer* document could get through. I used my laptop to create a very official looking *laissez-passer*, with logos of the Haitian Ministry of Health, Partners in Health and Yéle. Once that was printed and taped to the windows of each water tanker, the fleet was on its way. There was no roadblock, but at least we were prepared.

A few days later, I was back in Haiti and accompanied the water trucks on a number of deliveries. We arrived at a hospital that had been transformed into a cholera treatment center operated by Médecins Sans Frontières (Doctors Without Borders). The small facility was now operating well beyond capacity. In every room, hallway, and public space there were people lying on cots, benches and the floor, with anxious relatives hovering nearby. In an outdoor area behind the hospital, two large tents had been set up and these were also filled; some patients were in cots, but most were lying on the ground. It was like a scene from Dante's Inferno, complete with the sound of people wailing as a loved one died in front of them. Doctors and nurses were overwhelmed as they tried to help as many as they could. The situation was both heartbreaking and chaotic.

While our role in responding to the cholera epidemic was minor, Yéle was one of the first NGOs to provide daily deliveries of water in the Artibonite Valley and was the largest regular supplier there for several weeks.

Before long, cholera broke out in Port-au-Prince. We imported 40,000 bars of soap, 50,000 bottles of hand sanitizer, and 2 million water purification tablets, and began to deploy our Yéle Corps workers distributing these items tent by tent in the camps. The workers, who received training from Partners in Health, also spoke to camp residents about basic prevention techniques and gave demonstrations of proper hand washing.

DNA testing of the cholera bacteria and five independent scientific studies, which included some of the world's leading cholera epidemiologists, have definitively concluded that the cholera inadvertently brought to Haiti by the UN peacekeepers spread as a result of inadequate sanitation at a UN facility. But the world's largest humanitarian organization has refused to accept responsibility or to issue an apology to the people of Haiti. The UN can rightly invoke humanity's collective righteous indignation in response to all kinds of injustices and human rights violations around the world, but their moral authority will remain under a cloud until this matter is resolved. No organization can unwittingly release a disease that launches what became, at the time, the world's worst and fastest spreading cholera epidemic and then pretend they had nothing to do with it.

Time to go

One year after the earthquake, and six years after having co-founded Yéle with Wyclef and Jerry, it was time for me to leave the organization. I resigned at the end of February, 2011. It was not an easy decision. But I felt Yéle was never going to recover from the accusations that dogged us. I wanted to create a new NGO on my own, the story of which follows in the next chapter.

A year after my departure, Yéle shut its doors. The offices in both New York and Port-au-Prince were closed and all programs ceased to operate. There is talk of trying to revive the operation in Haiti. But while I wish them well, I will not be part of that venture. I remain committed to working in Haiti, but following a new path.

4

GREEN GLORY:

*Working With Small-scale Farmers to Plant Trees
and Improve Agriculture*

HAITI, 2009. Richard St. Barbe Baker, to whom I have dedicated this book, was an early mentor. I met this forester, author, and conservationist while I was a university student in London, England, in the late 1970s. He spent a lifetime helping to restore and maintain what he called "the green glory of the forests of the earth," and he was a pioneer in taking forestry from the confines of a professional discipline to a movement that involved entire communities. With a lifetime of practical examples of work to choose from, it was his early experience in Africa that particularly inspired me. St. Barbe, as he was called by his friends and colleagues, had been assistant conservator of forests in Kenya in the early 1920s. Concerned that the colonial government of which he was a part was cutting down huge swaths of trees without any corresponding effort to reforest, he enlisted the native Kikuyu to form a volunteer tree planting organization that became known as the "Men of the Trees." What set St. Barbe apart from other foresters was his ability to get the voluntary cooperation of local people by tapping into their culture. With the Kikuyu, that meant creating a secret society of tree planters who took part in a ritual dance initiation. Wearing full war regalia and carrying shields and spears, they pledged to serve as "forest scouts" by planting trees and protecting the forests.

From the moment I first set foot in Haiti, there was no question that, regardless of the initial focus of my work, it had to include a contribution to reforesting the country. Exactly how that would happen was unclear. Two early experiments, one in forestry and the second in agriculture, were each failures, albeit instructive: sometimes our biggest mistakes can lead to the most ground-breaking ideas.

The experiment in forestry that I undertook in 2005 centered on forming a national coalition of Haitian environmental NGOs to establish a series of tree nurseries across the country. This effort fell apart quickly, when, at the first sight of potential funding, one of the NGOs tried to take it over for their own financial benefit. Two lessons came from this failure. First, take care in choosing your partners, as one wrong step can create problems before you even get started. The second lesson came from the collective know-how I gleaned from the NGOs that had participated in some twenty years of planting trees in Haiti: it was clear that the only successful ventures involved working with small-scale, or smallholder, farmers.

The 2008 agricultural experiment was called "Together for Haiti," described in Chapter 2. Following the food crisis earlier that year, I had formed a coalition of like-minded organizations to work as a team to provide food, create jobs, and support local agriculture. The project itself was mostly a failure, except for the small and successful pilot program that involved providing high quality seeds to smallholder farmers. A simple thing to do, but it had a significant impact on the farmers, because they had never been able to afford the higher-yield seed that would bring them a corresponding higher income. In the brief time spent with these farmers, I was surprised to learn that they received no support of any kind from the government. Having grown up in the rural Canadian West, we took the government-run agricultural extension service for granted. I simply assumed that all farmers had a support system. But I quickly learned that most farmers in Haiti had never in their lifetime had a visit from the Ministry of Agriculture.

And then along came the Timberland Company. Wyclef had a commercial endorsement deal with this popular line of footwear and outdoor apparel. In early 2009, the company expressed interest in extending their involvement with Wyclef to supporting tree planting in Haiti through Yéle.

Timberland first proposed establishing a park in Port-au-Prince, drawing on their tradition of creating and improving urban green spaces using teams of local volunteers in various parts of the world. I countered by suggesting that the desperate need for trees in Haiti was so far beyond the scale of a park that the company might want to consider something on a larger scale. I shared a copy of a concept paper I had just written on tree planting and environmental restoration in Haiti that had been commissioned by a US foundation. To my delight, they were immediately receptive and asked me to come up with a proposal.

It is one thing to be forever pushing and advocating for something, but how often does a major corporation, particularly one with a reputation for being an industry leader in environmental and social responsibility, respond with "Yes!" followed by "How?"?

Agroforestry experiment

Three disasters in Haiti: the global food crisis in early 2008, the set of four storms in late summer of 2008, and the devastating 2010 earthquake, collectively resulted in a blizzard of papers with plans for helping Haiti recover. These papers were generated by a dazzling array of research organizations, think-tanks, governments, NGOs, institutions, and consulting companies. I eagerly read many of these documents. But in almost all of them, I was shocked to discover that there were two key issues missing: agriculture and trees. All the papers dealt with job creation, improving education, investing in infrastructure, addressing corruption, and increasing security. And while they might have had a sentence or two bemoaning the lack of trees or a paragraph on the sad state of agriculture, neither issue was a focus of their recommendations for helping the country recover. One notable exception was an excellent paper by Robert Maguire for the United States Institute of Peace called "Haiti After the Donors' Conference: A Way Forward," which dealt with agriculture and trees at length.

To me, it is glaringly obvious that, while the other problems must all be addressed in tandem, it would be complete folly to ignore the fundamental challenges of Haiti's lack of trees and the sorry state of the country's agricultural sector. With less than 2 percent of tree cover left—one recent estimate sets the figure as low as 1.4 percent—the country is moving from "tropical" to "tropical desert." Every major storm sends rain cascading down hillsides completely denuded of trees, resulting in untold damage from flooding. Topsoil has been washed away, leaving rocks perched on top of hard, baked subsoil. In agricultural terms, Haiti went from being largely self-sufficient in producing its own food in the mid-1980s, to now importing 58 percent of the food it consumes. This trend was matched by the decline of farm income, massive migration to the cities, and a dependence on food imports. Even with these pressures, two-thirds of the workforce is employed in agriculture, according to a 2011 World Bank report. I will never be convinced that it makes sense for a poor country like Haiti to spend an average of 80 percent of its export earnings to pay for imported food, when there exists a vast and capable reserve of smallholder farmers, who, if they were to receive just a little bit of technical assistance, could go back to producing much of the country's food, while increasing employment and income levels in the balance.

The lack of trees and the sorry state of agriculture are closely interconnected. As farm income declined beginning in the mid-1980s, more farmers turned to cutting down trees to produce charcoal for the increasing urban population. Already decreased to 5 percent by then, tree cover was further reduced over the next two decades to its current 2 percent or less. Fewer trees meant more farms were abandoned as entire watersheds collapsed or shrank, one after the other, throughout the country. And when a watershed is compromised, rivers dry up and ground water is greatly depleted. Irrigation becomes more difficult, and sometimes impossible, in a climate in which water is required to grow most crops.

As I set out to respond to the Timberland challenge, it was clear to me that for any plan to work, it had to be based on a combination of agriculture and tree planting, the discipline known as agroforestry. In the early 1980s, Richard St. Barbe Baker had introduced me to one of the worlds' leading authorities on agroforestry, Zhu Zhaohua, from the Chinese Academy of Forestry. I subsequently hosted Prof. Zhu on a tour of Canada in 1985, and the images he showed of food crops interspersed with trees caused a sensation at the time, as the extent of China's use of agroforestry was largely unknown in the West. Those images had a profound impact on me, and I now drew on that inspiration in a very pragmatic way.

The challenge was not how to combine planting trees and growing food crops; it was how to introduce the idea in a practical manner to farmers. Just asking them to plant trees was not enough of an incentive, even with an education component to teach the value of trees in stabilizing and improving the soil, helping to increase water retention, and so on. I consulted with Wangari Maathai, the founder of the Green Belt Movement and winner of the 2004 Nobel Peace Prize, whom I had originally met through St. Barbe, and who had become a good friend. In her successful program in Kenya, women grew trees and received incremental payments once the trees were planted and until they reached maturity. But I felt this would not work in Haiti, because we did not have the organizational capacity to monitor the trees as Wangari did with her Green Belt Movement.

Finally, a simple idea presented itself: why not ask farmers to volunteer to grow the trees in exchange for an agricultural service that would help them significantly increase their food crop yields by receiving better crop seeds, tools, and training? Their work to grow the trees would be paid for through the additional income they received as a result of higher yields.

At first this seemed too simple. Surely this was already being done. I asked around in Haiti, and there was no program of this kind. I checked with various international sources, and no one was aware of an existing operation based on this model. I am still sure it has been done elsewhere, but to date, I have not been able to find an example of this particular concept having been implemented.

However good the idea, it would not have moved from theory to practice had it not been for a young Haitian agronomist named Timote Georges. Suzie Sylvain, a Yéle colleague who had been a vital part of our organization since its inception, introduced me to an organization called Trees for the Future. Their program director, Ethan Budiansky, subsequently introduced me to Timote, who was the Country Director for Trees for the Future on the ground in Haiti. Both Ethan and Timote would become critical to the success of the new agroforestry program.

In mid 2009, before we formed a working partnership, Timote took me to see one of the tree nurseries he had created and was currently operating with the involvement of smallholder farmers. Located in the Artibonte Valley north of Port-au-Prince, this was exactly what I had envisioned: totally off the grid, extremely simple in operation, based entirely on organic principles, and run by local farmers. The only thing missing was the incentive component, linking it to food crops. When I explained that concept to Timote, he immediately embraced it, and in a matter of hours we had the whole program outlined.

I explained that we wanted to start a pilot program in the farming area outside Gonaïves, and that we would like to build an entirely new operation from scratch and not try and adapt any existing nurseries that Timote was already implementing. This was not a hard sell: Timote was keen to try this new idea. He was, in turn, backed by Ethan on the US side and together we set out to experiment with this new model. Gonaïves was chosen because of Yéle's years of activity there, and the fact that the city had been devastated by the 2008 floods, made worse because of the lack of tree cover surrounding the city.

Within a month, Yéle Haiti and Trees for the Future had joined forces to create "Yéle Vert," incorporating the French word for "green." The resulting community-based agroforestry program combined tree planting and sustainable agriculture in a way that would improve rural livelihoods, increase food production, and contribute to restoring the environment. With input from Timote and Ethan, I prepared an extensive document describing the proposed rollout of the program, along with a detailed multi-year budget, and we presented the plan to Timberland.

Nothing would have happened past this point had it not been for Jeff Swartz, the creative and dynamic president and CEO of Timberland. He is the third generation of the Swartz family to lead the company, his grandfather Nathan having started its predecessor in 1952. The company was subsequently sold in late 2011, but two years of Jeff's support was enough to ensure the continuing engagement of senior management.

Jeff's early endorsement of the overall concept set things in motion in 2009, but it was up to Margaret Morey-Reuner, senior manager for values marketing at Timberland, to make it work.

NGOs generally look to corporate sponsors to hand over money and, from that point on, to stay out of their business. This had certainly been my own approach over the years. But from the outset, it was different with Timberland. Through the involvement of both Jeff and Margaret, each in different roles, it was made clear that this was not their company's philosophy. Timberland had a very different, hands-on approach, and a very different reason for being involved. Most companies, with motives ranging from greenwashing to a genuine commitment to the environment, ultimately focus on the public relations value of their relationship with an NGO when it comes to something like planting trees. I was only to learn years later that Timberland had a very different reason: they were considering opening a manufacturing operation in Haiti and wanted to make sure, before taking any steps in that direction, that they could make a real and tangible contribution to restoring the environment. They could not justify setting up shop in a country with such a denuded environment if they were not first convinced that they could make some contribution to restoring that environment.

They were also launching a new line of Earthkeepers footwear, with US$2 from the sale of each pair of shoes or boots going to support their two tree planting programs, the new one in Haiti and the other already underway in China. I have to admit being absolutely thrilled when I first picked up an Earthkeepers boot in a Timberland store and saw the Yéle Haiti logo on the inside of the tongue. It is one thing to deal with all the legal paperwork, mockups of artwork, and marketing strategies, but quite another to walk into a store and see the real deal.

If I had any advice to offer other NGOs when approaching a corporate sponsor to underwrite environmental activities—or any other form of non-profit service for that matter—it would be to look for a company that has a business reason for supporting you. Any time you can find a sponsor that is engaged in philanthropy that ultimately affects their corporate bottom line, as was the case with Timberland, you will have a true partner and not just a source of funding.

Timberland was also the driving force that transformed Yéle Vert into a self-financing operation. It would have been an effective agroforestry program that lasted only as long as external funding kept flowing, but Timberland was key to turning it into a self-financing and farmer-managed operation, designed to function effectively long after the funding stopped. This they did by introducing a business discipline which, when combined with an NGO capacity to engage farmers at the local level, ultimately created something with real potential to transform farming in Haiti. More details on this later; meanwhile, back to how it all got started.

In October 2009, we signed an agreement between Yéle Haiti and Timberland, in which the latter agreed to be the sponsor and partner for the new Yéle Vert program. In a second agreement, Yéle Haiti hired Trees for the Future as the subcontractor responsible for implementing the program. I had overall responsibility, Timote headed up day-to-day operations on site, and Margaret and Ethan worked with me on the administrative details.

Just as Richard St. Barbe Baker had created a secret society of tree planters in Kenya in the early 1920s, drawing on local cultural traditions, so Timote came up with the idea of basing Yéle Vert on existing local farming associations. Almost every smallholder farmer throughout Haiti is a member of one or another informal local association. This is a phenomenon not only among farmers: almost every one of the working poor throughout Haiti is a member of a professional association. It was Timote who recommended that Yéle Vert begin by inviting the farmer associations, and not the farmers themselves, to take part. As a result of this important recognition of the existing local structure, twenty-five associations in the farming area northwest of Gonaïves immediately signed up as word spread that this program was respectful of the local traditions and worth a try.

The first innovation of Yéle Vert was to get farmers to plant trees by "paying" them in the form of an agricultural service that increased food crop yields. The second was to organize the program as a network of existing farmer associations, so that it was seen as a natural extension of the way in which farmers had always organized themselves.

In December 2009, we rented the land for the main tree nursery in a small farming community called Mapou, about fifteen minutes from the outskirts of Gonaïves. Land was donated for a second, smaller nursery in another nearby farming community called Rofilie. The plan was to eventually construct six of these smaller nurseries, all on land donated by the community. The tree nurseries had to be disbursed in this way so as to be close enough to the plots of participating farmers that they could transport the trees by wheelbarrow. The overall operation, and all trainings, would be conducted from the main nursery. To facilitate these activities, plans were made to build two structures: a three-room office and a traditional *choucoune*, which has a thatched roof supported by poles and open sides allowing ventilation. The office was for administration and storage of seeds and equipment, while the *choucoune* was for training sessions and regular meetings of the farmers.

We all agreed that the first tree seeds in this pilot operation would be planted starting on January 15, 2010, which turned out to be unrealistic because of the earthquake a few days earlier. But because the earthquake did not affect the Gonaïves area directly, the planting was delayed by only a few weeks.

Yéle Vert began as a program under the auspices of Yéle Haiti, but success brought with it ever increasing management demands over time. It became clear that, in order for this program to reach its true potential, it needed to become a stand-alone operation. Once again, it was Timberland that played a critical role by encouraging us to create a new NGO that would continue the program. Out of that discussion was born the "Smallholder Farmers Alliance." As this book goes to print, we have formed not one, but two new organizations. Smallholder Farmers Alliance is the new Haitian NGO that is now managing and guiding the agroforestry program, acknowledging the critical role played by Yéle Haiti and Trees for the Future, but moving ahead, independent of both. I serve as president of Smallholder Farmers Alliance and Timote is Country Director; we are both co-founders.

The second organization involves the incorporation of the farmers who implemented the pilot program into a separate agroforestry cooperative called "Alyans Ti Plantè-Gonaïves," using the Creole for Smallholder Farmers Alliance. As of May, 2012, there are now 1,000 farm households that are members, through their respective associations; this translates to some 2,000 farmers, when considering that most farms involve the equal participation of both husband and wife. Between them, the farmers in Alyans Ti Plantè-Gonaïves have approximately 1,500 hectares of land (just over 3,700 acres), and together, they now operate a total of eight tree nurseries—one main nursery plus seven smaller community nurseries—with a combined annual output of one million trees a year.

Meanwhile, Timberland opened a shoe factory in Haiti in late 2011, located in the Northeastern city of Ouanaminthe.

Global food fight

I was raised in a small prairie town in the Canadian province of Saskatchewan, surrounded by farms. It was an idyllic place to grow up, with waving fields of grain, mostly wheat, stretching to the horizon in every direction. The average size of farms in that area is just over two square miles (1,280 acres). I took for granted that farming always involved tractors, trucks, combines, synthetic fertilizer, and a plethora of chemical-based herbicides and pesticides. To us, this was just the natural order of things; we did not know it was the quintessential definition of industrial farming.

Now I understand that the farming community in which I was raised was part of a significant global phenomenon. Humanity bases two-thirds of its diet on three grains: corn (also known as maize), rice, and wheat; and the livestock we eat also depends largely on grains for feed. What is truly amazing is that since the early 1960s, grain production around the world nearly tripled, as the world population doubled.

Had grain production not increased so dramatically, there would not have been enough food to feed the world; and this increase in food production was possible only because of industrial farming.

But it was not until I started working in Haiti that I thought about the consequences of industrial farming. It seemed a noble thing that a solution had been found to feed the world, and that my forbearers and the farmers I grew up with were part of this effort. Canada is among the six countries that, between them, supply 90 percent of global grain exports, the others being the United States, France, Australia, Argentina, and Thailand. It took a dramatic event in Haiti to tear away the veil concealing a jerry-rigged, dysfunctional, and inefficient system, into which the unsuspecting farmers of Saskatchewan had been unwittingly drawn.

There is nothing quite so effective in garnering public attention as mass protests and riots in dozens of countries at the same time, all in response to the same situation. The global food crisis in early 2008 was a popular uprising in response to a major rise in food prices. The bill came due for a dysfunctional global food system that relied too much on industrial farming, and millions upon millions of the poor were being asked to pick up the tab. They said "no!" in a collective roar, loud enough to reverberate around the world.

In Haiti there were violent riots throughout the country in March and April of 2008 to protest food prices. President René Préval sacked his prime minister and cabinet not long after protesters tried to storm the presidential palace. While a new prime minister was appointed some months later, most of the previous cabinet was quietly returned to office after the protests died down.

So how did the global food crisis come about? First, some background: The tripling of world grain production since the early 1960s did not happen by accident. The economists, planners, and politicians who were re-drawing the postwar map of the world in the 1950s and early 60s saw the need to restructure global agriculture in order to make it more productive. Approximately half the world's workers at that time were farmers, but the majority of the food was already being grown by the minority involved in large scale industrial farming. This had the advantage of producing food more cheaply than the small-scale farmers who constituted the majority could do. Steps were taken to focus research, resources, and regulations to support industrial farming, and then to export the increased grain production to poor and underdeveloped countries, whose farmers could not afford to invest in industrial methods. Over the course of forty years, the huge increase in grain production was almost entirely the result of increased support for industrial farming. The good news was increased grain production. The bad news was that, behind the scenes, the original concept was flawed from the outset and matters kept getting worse over forty years until the dam burst.

There is, to my mind, a very clear and necessary role for industrial farming. But it is not the sole answer to feeding the world, at the expense of smallholder farmers. At first, industrial farming seemed like a simple and elegant formula for providing food for a growing world population. Modern, efficient, logical. Take the burden off poor countries by growing cheap food elsewhere and exporting it to them so that their rural poor could abandon farming and move to the cities, buy cheap imported food, and become part of the urban industrial model that, supposedly, would help improve economies everywhere.

It was not long, however, before unforeseen problems with this formula surfaced. The smallholder farmers who lost their incomes because they could not compete with cheap imported food moved in record numbers to cities that were not able to offer them jobs. The result was often increased poverty. In order to keep local food prices down, it became necessary to lower import tariffs in the poor counties receiving the cheap food from abroad. But this meant reduced tax income to run those governments. At the same time, high tariffs were maintained in most of the countries growing the food, because they would otherwise face unfair competition from poor countries. And when it seemed that the exported food would not be cheap enough, the rich countries began to tap their own taxpayers to give ever larger subsidies to their industrial farmers. But that would only

Author photo.

The 2,000 farmers in the pilot agroforestry cooperative of the Smallholder Farmers Alliance (SFA) currently grow one million trees a year in eight nurseries. They plant the trees on their own farms and community land.

William Charles Moss.

SFA agroforestry cooperative member Jacqueline Castin, shown here holding the fruit from a papaya tree she planted on her farm near Mapou. Jacqueline sells the papaya to supplement her farm income.

Sebastian Petion.

Rigaud Joseph, shown here with his sorghum crop in 2011. Farmers in the Small-holder Farmers Alliance cooperative receive seed, training, and tools that help them increase their crop yields by an average of 40 to 50 percent.

Author photo.

Children of farmer members attending an environmental education class. Full time teacher Rosie Despergnes (left, holding leaf) is assisted by noted Haitian environmentalist Jane Wynne (right), who is also an SFA board member.

Sebastian Petion.

Children of farmers are shown here helping to fill some of the 700,000 bags used each year to transplant tree seedlings into plastic bags filled with a soil-compost mixture.

Timote Georges.

Cooperative farmer members planting a "living fence" of trees to define their property and keep out wandering livestock. Fences made of posts and barbed wire are too expensive for most smallholder farmers in Haiti.

Sebastian Petion.

Author Hugh Locke with Timote Georges (center), co-founder of the Smallholder Farmers Alliance and our Country Director in Haiti. We are conferring with Thanael Jean (left), one of the agroforestry technicians with the SFA cooperative near Gonaïves.

Louis Dario Louis.

Farmer members of the SFA agroforestry cooperative near Gonaïves grow one million trees a year in eight nurseries and then transport the seedlings, usually by wheelbarrow, to their nearby farms and community land for transplanting.

work if the poor countries promised never to give their own farmers any subsidies, a general policy that was reinforced by making the removal of all farm subsidies a condition for continued development funding from the rich countries. And because these actions all seemed profoundly unfair, they were collectively given a name that meant the opposite of what was actually happening: the whole system became known as "trade liberalization," when, in reality, it meant systematic trade *restriction*.

Over time, what could originally be outlined in an elevator ride became a book. The book became many volumes. The volumes became an entire library. Every time there was a problem, more regulations were added to prop up the system, so that eventually the entire collection was so large that nobody knew exactly what all the rules were. Here was a complex system rather like a computer in need of regular updates to guard against viruses. But suddenly, with little warning, the computer crashes. The original formula in which industrial farms would feed the world had been patched up so many times, that it was finally unable to correct itself in response to a set of conditions that caused a total systems failure known as the "global food crisis" of 2008.

There was no one trigger for the food crisis. The real story is complex. Start with core numbers: the world's population is now growing faster and is close to consuming more food than the world can produce, because the increase in the yields of industrial farming peaked years ago. Add to this an increase in the cost of the fossil fuel needed to run industrial farm machinery and operate the ships that take the food to markets around the world. Then factor in the growing prosperity of countries like China, where people are eating more meat, which in turn requires more grain to be diverted to livestock. Add to this the significant increase in the use of biofuels for cars and the resulting loss of arable land from food production. And to top it all off, legalized gambling by investors who speculate in the agricultural futures market. Without even considering the significant long-term impact on the environment and human health, this set of factors came together to create the perfect storm in food prices.

Whatever the immediate causes for the food crisis, the bigger story is that the entire global agricultural sector has not been managed in humanity's collective best interest. Industrial agriculture was given every advantage and forced to carry the burden for generating most of the world's food, while hundreds of millions of smallholder farmers had much of their support withdrawn. Simultaneously, regulations and laws were put in place to systematically reduce smallholder output and force them to leave farming. Thus, smallholder farmers—who still constitute close to one third of the world's workers—are not being given the opportunity to help bridge the gap, even as industrial farming has reached the limits of its capacity to produce. This is the situation that caused the global food crisis of 2008. Because of its artificial structure favoring the minority and working actively against the majority, the agricultural sector had become too complex and was unable to respond and adjust to the set of conditions that triggered the crisis.

While the food crisis is no longer on the front page, there is no question that the underlying conditions have not gone away. We still need to grow more food: by 2050 we will have added the current equivalent of two Chinas to the global population. Ahead lay two forks in the road, each pointing to a potential solution: one road leads to a new green revolution with supercharged genetically engineered seeds (commonly referred to as genetically modified organisms, or GMOs) that will significantly increase the yield of existing industrial farms. The other leads to a smallholder farm revolution that will finally support the world's 900 million currently marginalized smallholder farmers, enabling them to improve their sustainable and ecologically friendly practices to meet growing global demand.

In reality, both roads have a place. But from my vantage point there is nothing resembling an even playing field between the two. Powerful forces are already lining up behind a new GMO green revolution and discounting even the possibility of discussing a smallholder farm revolution. If the latter are considered at all, they are seen as merely incidental players, to be enlisted to ensure that the GMO juggernaut achieves maximum global coverage.

Meet the farmers

I would like to introduce you to one family in order to give you an understanding of the life of smallholder farmers in Haiti.

Gustave and his wife Rosemary (I am not sharing their family name) and their seven children live on a farm near the tiny community of Rofilie. Gustave is fifty-three years old, and Rosemary is forty-eight. The children range from three to the eldest, Guibert, who is nineteen. Gustave and Rosemary, assisted by Guibert and other family members, are equal partners in farming their one hectare of land, half of which they own, while the other half is rented. The family also includes two older women, Rosemary's mother and an aunt of Gustave, bringing the total count to eleven people in this farm household.

They live together in a two-room house with a cement floor, wood frame walls, plastered inside and out with packed earth painted light yellow, and a corrugated tin roof. There is one door, painted turquoise blue with a red frame, and three windows without glass, but which can be closed using wooden shutters painted to match the door. The roof extends over the front of the house to form a sheltered area. The front room has a table in the middle with a single exposed light bulb suspended over it, power being supplied by a jerry-rigged link to a nearby power line—and it is likely that no bill ever arrives for this service. There is also a cabinet in the front room with a display of artificial flowers and several pieces of exuberant porcelain. The room is immaculately clean, as is the second room, with its several beds and almost no space between them.

The house opens onto a courtyard of hard, packed earth, bordered on one side by a storage building, of the same construction as the house, and a pigeon coop. The other two sides of the space are defined by a fence made of woven palm fronds. Again, all is clean and well organized. In the courtyard and the covered area in front of the house are a number of metal and plastic chairs, as this is where the family spends most of their time when at home. This outdoor area also serves as the kitchen. Set into the courtyard surface is a small charcoal pit with an open metal structure that holds one pot at a time for cooking.

Upon enquiring about bathroom facilities, I am informed by Gustave, with a sweep of his hand aimed at the outdoor area beyond the compound that, depending on which direction you want to go, you will find the "bathroom." Bathing is done in a large metal bowl in a sheltered area near the compound.

In a second adjoining courtyard, there is a chicken coop built by Gustave, with six chickens on three levels, each enclosed with wire netting. The structure is supported by four corner posts that raise the whole coop several feet off the ground. An ingenious system of recycled plastic pipes delivers water to each level from a storage tank on the top. Also in this second courtyard is a cow that the oldest son Guibert is responsible for milking each day.

It is a short walk from the family compound to the first part of their farm. The field is bordered on one side by community land owned collectively by the neighbors, on which several cows are grazing contentedly. On this morning, the perfect stillness is broken by American rock music blaring from a nearby house.

The farm itself consists of two separate fields together measuring one hectare (just under 2.5 acres). The first field is a rectangular space divided into several sections by a method dating back to the colonial period, when plantation slaves were allowed to grow food for themselves on similar small plots. This farm, like those during slave times, represents a particular type of intensive agriculture that reminded me of the market gardens of my youth. On this one field are onions, eggplant, and corn, each growing within squares defined by a ridge of earth about a foot high. These ridges allow the field to be flooded, one square at a time, to irrigate the crops. On the second field, a few minutes away, are the same smaller plots; but in this case, they are all planted with beans.

In this area of Haiti, most farming involves irrigation. As you drive down the dirt roads that connect the rural communities, you come across small, one-story pumping stations that were originally installed during the Duvalier era, and are now kept running by the farmers. They have a knack for keeping the ancient machinery going in the absence of any government help. The pumping stations draw water from underground sources and feed it into a network of hand-dug irrigation channels, most no more than two feet deep, that crisscross the whole area for hundreds of miles. The entire operation, other than the pumping stations, is managed by hand. When the water needs to be re-directed, earth is shoveled to plug up one route while the embankment is broken to open another. Once off the roads, movement through the fields is mostly accomplished by walking along these irrigation embankments.

Gustave and Rosemary have been part of Yéle Vert, and now the Smallholder Farmers Alliance, since its inception in 2010. Touring their farm in early 2012, there is clear evidence of the trees they have planted on their land. The first field is surrounded on two sides by a "living fence" that has been built up over the last two years by planting a combination of jatropha bushes and siwel trees. Jatropha is a thorny bush that helps to keep livestock out, while the siwel has very long, thin branches that are bent down and woven into the jatropha to form a very dense enclosure. In addition to keeping out cattle and other animals, living fences are very important for avoiding land disputes. When you have two fields next to each other under similar cultivation, the exact border can be hard to maintain. This is where living fences come in, and they are significantly cheaper than those made of posts and barbed wire, which are too expensive for most farmers in Haiti.

While the living fence was clearly an asset, what excited me in touring this farm were the six papaya trees in the middle of the field. These had been grown as part of Yéle Vert and transplanted here by Gustave and Rosemary in May of 2010. The trees were now about twelve feet high, and the reason they worked here was that the foliage began about seven feet above ground, and did not disrupt or shade the crops. From seed to first fruit is about one year, and as of January 2012, these six trees had each produced an average of eighty large papayas, enough to significantly add to their overall farm income, as the fruit, beyond what the family could eat, was sold.

Farmers in this part of Haiti grow three crops a year. Depending on the arrival of seasonal rain, the crops are usually planted in April, July, and December. Once stable and predictable, local weather patterns have become much more erratic over the past decade and planting is often delayed by several weeks or even a month. This causes problems for the farmers because it delays income and cuts down the time needed to prepare the land between crops. All three seasons include the planting of vegetables and corn, while sorghum is planted in April and beans in December.

Typical of the 1,000 farm households taking part in the agroforestry cooperative, Gustave and Rosemary farm as partners. They farm together and they both volunteer to tend the tree nurseries. In return for that volunteer service, they receive trees to plant on their land and seeds for their food crops. Visiting their field in January 2012, the onions had been provided through the cooperative, as were the papaya trees and the living fence; their second field was planted with beans provided by the program.

While the partnership of husband and wife covers the operation of the farms, Rosemary's role in dealing with the household finances is typical of most farm households: she is responsible for selling all the produce at the outdoor market in Gonaïves and handles the money for the household.

Gustave and Rosemary are also typical of other farmers involved the cooperative. Finally able to get higher quality seed, some training, and good quality hoes and shovels, their yields increased and income along with it. To give a specific example, their sorghum harvest in July 2011, with seed provided by the cooperative, had a 50 percent higher yield than any they had ever had. Out of their overall operation on two fields and three seasons a year, sorghum accounts for close to half their annual income. The higher yield of sorghum meant that the family was able to send two of their children to high school. This marked the first time in the family's extended history when anyone was able to attend high school. Gustave was fairly bursting with pride as he told me of this development. And it was interesting that he and his wife choose a daughter as well as a son, rather than two sons, for this privilege, as the culture definitely favors boys over girls.

Gustave has an additional role as a member of the farmers' committee. This is another of Timote's very important innovations. He realized that the farmers had to own the program from the outset. So he had the farmers identify one leader from each of the twenty-five participating farmer associations and began training them to oversee both the tree nurseries and the agricultural service.

The resulting farmers' committee is responsible for canvassing the other farmers to find out what trees they want to grow and where they will be planting them. This ensures that the use of the trees has been predetermined by the farmers themselves. The committee then has to find a source of tree seeds, and, guided by Timote, negotiate the purchase price. They oversee the planting schedule and care of the nurseries by the other farmers. This is followed by organizing the entire community at planting time when the trees are taken from the nurseries and transplanted on fields and community land. With one million trees a year now being grown by the eight nurseries, this is no small undertaking.

The second major task of the farmers' committee relates to food crops. They canvas all the farmers as to what seeds they need and in what quantity. Then the committee, again guided by Timote, must find a source for that seed and negotiate the price. Once the seeds are planted, the committee goes regularly to inspect the growing crops. Any problems are reported back to Timote and his small team of agronomists and technicians and they help formulate a response. In the case of insect control, this usually takes the form of a spray made from the neem tree. This tree grows throughout Haiti, and the leaves are pressed to extract oil that can be mixed with garlic, peppers and other natural ingredients to make a spray. Different combinations are tested until an effective solution is found.

The farmers' committee consists entirely of volunteer farmers who are members of the cooperative. The small paid staff of agronomists serve as a resource to the committee, but they are not members. In this way the farmers themselves become experts in every aspect of running the program and have an ownership stake in the operation. That would never have been the case if we had followed the typical top-down management style of most NGO programs.

Tree portraits

Now that you have met some of the farmers, I would like to introduce you to five of the typical trees grown in our nurseries. It is one thing to say that the trees are grown for their fruit, timber, and for fodder, but what does that actually mean? In Haiti, there are close to two dozen indigenous tree species, but these five have been chosen by the farmers as most important.

My favorite by far is called *Moringa oleifera*, known locally as *doliv* or *benzoliv*. This tree is both elegant and tough. While most trees are initially grown in seed beds and then allowed to mature in plastic bags until transplanting, the *Moringa* is so hardy that it is grown in the ground and then pulled up to be transplanted. Not dug up with care to keep soil on the roots. Rather, pulled out like a common weed and planted in a field, where it begins to grow again very quickly. The result is astonishing. Within a year the young tree can reach fifteen feet. The leaves are very delicate, each a composite made up of many smaller leaves, arranged off a central stem.

The drought-resistant *Moringa* is considered one of the world's most useful trees, because almost every part can be used for nutrition, medicine, fodder, or water purification. The leaves have more protein per weight than beans, making it unique among all known tree species. The leaves can be eaten right off the tree, added to soup or rice, or dried and ground into a nutritious powder as a protein supplement to almost any other food. Although the *Moringa* grows in many tropical countries, it has not yet been sufficiently studied to verify its attributes. If an organization such as UNICEF or the World Food Programme were to one day endorse and begin using dried and ground Moringa leaves,

Haitian farmers could be major producers.

I spoke earlier about Gustave and Rosemary's papayas. In just three months, a papaya tree grown from seed can be transplanted to a field, and in a single year attains a height of twelve feet and produces around eighty large papayas. There can be as many as twenty fruit ripening on the tree at once—not modest little fruit, but huge papayas with an incredibly sweet flavor.

Jatropha curcas, known locally as *gwo medsiyen*, is actually a bush. I mentioned it earlier as a popular choice for living fences, as Gustave and Rosemary did on their farm. This is a scrappy bush that even its most ardent supporters could not call attractive. But it can flourish under the harshest conditions, and the large thorns make it ideally suited for keeping livestock out of fields. Many people know *Jatropha* for the small fruit that is pressed to extract biofuel. Despite the initial flurry of support for this process, it has never taken off in Haiti because harvesting on a commercial scale would require planting large plantations and not just hedgerows. Proponents of biofuel have pledged not to take over land currently being used to produce food, but it is difficult to imagine how that could be prevented if there were a viable market in Haiti for biofuel made from *Jatropha*.

And then there is *Cedrela odorata*, or *sèd*, Spanish cedar. An award for the tree most suited to one thing would surely go to this species, which produces perfect poles and planks. It has a single, straight trunk and few side branches, except for a modest flurry at the top. Within two years of planting, it can be harvested for use as a pole up to fourteen feet high. Wait three more years, and it will be large enough in girth for cutting into construction planks. It has the added feature that, when harvested, the *Cedrela* grows back from the root. A good example of how it is used is to be found in the family farm compound of another couple, Anouce and Idelia, who live near the rural community of Mapou. In November, 2010 they planted fifty *Cedrela* on their quarter-acre compound, along with five papaya—all of which they had helped to raise in the tree nursery cooperative in Mapou. The couple have already been harvesting the papaya and will be able to begin harvesting and selling the *Cedrela* trees later this year. Between the papaya and *Cedrela*, they will receive a reliable supplement to their income for years to come.

The *Citrus sinensis*, known locally as *oranj*, and in English as an orange tree, seems somehow very stately. It will not be rushed, and takes five years before it produces fruit. But it is worth the wait, because, once started, it will bear bountiful crops of oranges for several decades. The leaves are a glossy dark green and the flowers wonderfully fragrant. Its introduction to this part of Haiti is an experiment, as it is a native of more northerly regions near the coastal city of Cap-Haitien; but we see no reason why it should not be as successful in Gonaïves.

Nurturing the nurseries

The eight nurseries that form the core of the pilot operation of the Smallholder Farmers Alliance in Gonaïves are entirely off the grid. No electricity lines, no water from faucets, no tractors or other fuel-powered machinery, and no lights, the single exception being the main nursery, which has a generator to power two laptop computers and an internet connection. When you walk into any of the nurseries you see thousands of tree seedlings, either in long rows of raised beds or in individual black plastic bags set in neat rows on the ground. Some trees are transplanted with just bare roots, but most are started in the raised beds and transplanted after a few months to individual dirt-filled black plastic bags, where they grow for a few more months until they are ready for transplanting onto the farmers' land.

An ongoing activity at all the nurseries throughout the year is preparing the soil and filling the bags. Try as I might to get the men involved, this is something that is done by women farmers and their children. My frequent participation in this task has failed to inspire any of the male farmers to help out. Men manage the process of sifting the soil through fine mesh and adding compost, while women and children then fill hundreds of thousands of 6-inch-high bags. It is a huge task in itself, apart from the work of transplanting the seedlings into the soil-filled bags.

Each nursery has a compost pile, the output of which is enhanced with manure from nearby farms. In addition to providing compost for each nursery, it is a practical training for farmers, who then create their own compost operation. Even on hot days you can see steam rising from the watering hole at the top of the compost piles. Protruding above the mound is the tall stake that extends downwards to the bottom and which is used to continually "stir" the pile to ensure the penetration of both air and water into its depths, ensuring that plant matter breaks down efficiently.

Despite all our "off the grid" procedures, we are still dependent on purchasing close to 700,000 black plastic bags a year, with the remaining 300,000 trees being grown for bare root transplanting. This constitutes the single largest non-personnel expenditure in the budget. We looked into recycling Haiti's ubiquitous 10-ounce plastic water pouches, but after extensive experimentation over two years, we found that only one species of tree would grow in them. *Swietenya macrophylla*, known locally as *acajou*, used for timber and fuel, was the only tree that grows successfully in the recycled pouches.

But now we have a program to recycle the black bags. Children collect them from the farmers after they are discarded, sort them, and receive a credit for the reusable bags. That credit is then exchanged for illustrated books which are paid for through the savings in purchasing new bags.

The books, in turn, are part of an environmental education program for the children of the farmers who operate each of the nurseries. A full-time teacher travels between the nurseries giving classes to the children. They learn through a range of activities, such as pressing strips of wet paper to make briquettes and learning songs incorporating tales of wildlife. This education component came about as a result of an oft-repeated request from the farmers shortly after the program began, and is now hugely popular.

Radical seed saving

Farmers the world over have traditionally saved seed from their grain and vegetable harvests in order to plant again the following year. Haitian farmers have the same tradition, but face two very real problems. First, it is often difficult for them to save enough money to initially purchase the better seeds that would give them higher yields; and when you start off with poor seed, you will be stuck with it every season as you save and replant. Better seed is not a reference to hybrids, but rather to open-pollinated seed for crops that have been grown for generations in Haiti and have adapted over time to the tropical climate. The second problem is the financial pressure to sell the entire crop at the end of the season in order to meet their family's needs, and then having to struggle to get the money together to buy new seed for the next planting season.

It is hard to believe, but the seemingly simple task of organizing our farmers to contribute a portion of each season's harvest to a community seed bank is a fundamentally radical step that, by definition, engages the Smallholder Farmers Alliance in a worldwide debate about the future of farming.

To put this debate into context, we need to step out from the fields of Haiti. The foundation for the debate was spelled out in the last years of the 18th century by the English scholar and economist Thomas Robert Malthus. He was the first to put forward a theory of population which states that the number of people in the world increases in a geometric ratio, while the food supply increases in an arithmetic ratio. Population, he predicted, would increase faster than food supply, and the result would eventually be famine, disease, or war.

Malthusian theory did not take into account other factors, such as lowered birth rates. But his lasting influence has to do with two lines on a graph: one line represents the global population and the other line is our food supply. In 1960, there were three billion people in the world and a projection that this number would double within thirty years. Total global agricultural output was not growing at the same rate, leading economists, policy makers, and politicians to propose a wholesale move to industrial farming as the answer. At the time, as mentioned earlier in this chapter, it was thought that a massive investment in industrial farming was the only possible way to double global food output during the same period that population doubled. While it may not have been the only option, it certainly did increase food production, and it unquestionably averted what would have been a major global catastrophe: population did not exceed food supply.

Now the two lines on the graph are once again getting perilously close. Charting the population line, the United Nations announced that the world population hit 7 billion in October, 2011. We are projected to be at 9.2 billion by 2050, an increase of more than two billion people from 2012. The problem is that the food production line has leveled off in recent years. Nearly 40 percent of the earth's land surface is already used for agriculture, and the UN's Food and Agriculture Organization (FAO) projects that 90 percent of the growth in crop production between now and 2050 will need to come from higher yields on existing farms. At the same time, they predict that developing countries will more than double their import of grains, because the majority of the population growth will be in countries that are not currently growing enough food to feed themselves.

It is industrial agriculture that has largely fed the world up to now, but it has reached its limit, both in terms of available land and the yields that can be achieved using hybrid seeds, synthetic fertilizers, herbicides, and pesticides. Today's equivalent of the economists, policy makers, and politicians who advocated for industrial farming in the 1960s are again pushing for the same kind of global intervention, but this time in favor of genetically modified seeds (GMOs): a "gene revolution." If the combination of hybrid seed and industrial farming was the answer in the 1960s, so goes the prevailing theory, then the worldwide introduction of GMOs to industrial farming is the answer to feeding 75 million more people a year.

An issue of this magnitude is worthy of more exploration before we get back to the fields of Haiti. First, what is the difference between a hybrid seed and a GMO seed? All grain and vegetable seed is either open-pollinated or hybrid. All GMO seeds are hybrids by definition, but not all hybrids are GMOs.

Open-pollinated is a term that refers to seeds that produce the same plant in successive generations. Pollination occurs with the help of either bees, birds, or wind. You plant the crop, save some of the seed from the harvest, and then use that saved seed to plant the next crop. The saved seed will result in a plant that is similar to the parent. Over long periods of time specific grains and vegetables will evolve and adapt to local conditions; but in the process, they remain stable; that is, the saved seed can be grown and will produce the same offspring.

Hybrid seeds are produced by crossing two parent varieties from the same species, as in one species of tomato being crossed with another. Hybrids are developed by plant breeders who are specialists in combining the best traits of separate varieties into new varieties that offer higher yields, greater resistance to disease, and more vigor. One variety of wheat, for example, might have a higher yield but the heavier seed tends to make it fall over. It is then crossed with a second variety of wheat that does not have such a high yield, but which has a stronger stem. The first generation offspring from these two varieties will then have both a high yield and a strong stem. However, the second generation will often revert to one or other of the parents and will not duplicate the positive first generation results. Greater uniformity is another valuable characteristic in developing hybrids, because it makes it easier to use machinery to harvest the resulting crops. Most farmers who plant hybrid seed purchase it each growing season and do not save any for the following season, either because the next generation of plants will not match the first, or because they have signed a contract with the company that produced the hybrid seeds which obliges the farmer not to save seeds for replanting.

Hybrid seeds combine genes from different varieties of the same species through controlled pollination, but it is still a natural process. GMOs could never be produced in nature, because it involves combining plant genes with those from animals, bugs, fungi, and viruses. This process of combining plant with non-plant genes can only be done in a laboratory by scientists. But by opening up the gene pool beyond just those from plants, researchers are able to come up with plant hybrids that are custom designed to meet all kinds of very specific criteria, particularly higher yields than were ever possible with traditional hybrids.

So what, you may ask, is all the fuss about? Why is there so much fear regarding GMOs in so many parts of the world? The reasons vary, and high on the list are concerns about the environmental and health ramifications. But there are also concerns that date back to the green revolution of the 1960s. As detailed above, the massive international investment in industrial agriculture that began at that time required a range of trade policies in order to work. These policies protected the countries producing food for export and ensured that the poor countries importing the food kept their import tariffs low and agreed not invest in smallholder farming. A good example is the US Congress passing of the Bumpers Amendment in 1986 to the Foreign Assistance Act, which bars the government from helping farmers in developing countries to increase the yields of crops that could compete with staple US exports to those same countries. Public policy in many rich nations also ensured that research money went into developing hybrids and the related synthetic fertilizers, herbicides, and pesticides that these hybrids need in order to produce maximum yields. In short, investment, regulations, and research were all lined up behind industrial farming, with the result that smallholder farmers the world over suffered the consequences. The orchestrated effort behind industrialized farming is fast transforming into a full symphony singing the praises of GMOs, with nary a dissonant note to be heard.

There is one key difference, however, between the industrialized farming strategy of old and the new worldwide expansion of GMOs currently underway. Unlike the original green revolution that backed industrial farming, the GMO revolution is being led by private companies that have taken out patents on their laboratory-generated seeds. These private companies are responsible for some 90 percent of the worldwide research in GMOs. By asking governments around the world to enact laws to protect their investment, they have created a situation whereby all farmers who use their GMO seeds will be breaking the law if they save seeds for replanting.

To put the issue into perspective, it is currently estimated that approximately 80 percent of all grain and vegetables grown commercially on farms of all sizes come from hybrid seeds. If you break down hybrid seed between conventional hybrids and GMOs, the GMO percentage of the overall total grain and vegetable production stood at 7 percent as of 2011. Many parts of the world, including more than a dozen developing countries, are now experimenting with planting GMOs, but so far some 90 percent of GMO use is concentrated in only four countries: the United States, Argentina, Brazil, and Canada. But the use of GMOs is doubling, on average, every year.

The world faces the very real challenge of how to feed two billion more people by 2050. We have already reached the limit of available arable land, and the capacity of that land to produce food is only enough to feed the current population, with a little to spare. One scenario is that GMOs will expand on their current trajectory and by 2015 will represent more than half of global grain and vegetable production. Then, if there is one bad harvest in a significant industrial farming area, investor speculation on the agricultural futures market could, as it has in the past, send food prices through the roof. In a world in which food is a commercial commodity, millions would starve as a result. And in this scenario, they would starve not because there is not enough food being produced, but because the food they need is grown in the wrong place and controlled by companies whose business is not to feed the starving, but to maximize shareholder returns.

I am not suggesting that industrial farming, hybrids—and even GMOs, moving forward—do not have a vital role to play. They are absolutely essential to feeding the world, and without them we would long ago have faced a human catastrophe of historic proportions. What I am suggesting is that we need a core change in the global agricultural paradigm that will diffuse the extreme polarization that currently exists between industrial and smallholder farming. We need to make room for more sustainable and ecologically friendly practices that benefit from the same kind of research, investment, trade regulations, and legal frameworks that are being extended to industrial farmers. The main beneficiaries of this change would be the 900 million smallholder farmers around the world who have been marginalized for generations, but who could easily begin to fill an important gap in the global food chain.

Ultimately, this whole issue goes back to Gustave and Rosemary and their sorghum harvest in July 2011. By volunteering to grow trees, they earned the high yield sorghum seed that was used to plant that crop, seed that came from a seed bank managed by the farmers' committee. Participating farmers receive seed for food crops at the beginning of each growing season, and then return the same amount when they harvest their crops. To get the seed bank started, and to regularly replenish it, we buy high quality open-pollinated, non-hybrid seed. Before any harvested seed is added to the bank, it is first checked by the committee. In this way the seed source for the community is maintained at a high level, resulting in an average of 40 to 50 percent higher yields. These increased yields are not only based on better seeds, but also better farming practices that includes the use of compost, not burning off plant remnants at the end of the season, and more controlled spacing between plants.

Gustave and Rosemary are like many other smallholder farmers. They save seeds from season to season; except that in their case, they are now doing so as part of a cooperative of other farmers and in a manner that increases their output and income. In common with hundreds of millions of other smallholder farmers worldwide, they have always planted non-hybrid seeds and have never used any chemical fertilizer. With a little training, better seeds, and a new spirit of community, a modest experiment in rural Haiti is being offered up as one contribution to the larger global food challenge.

It is often claimed that smallholder farmers benefit from higher yields when they switch to hybrid seeds. For the most part, those espousing this view have never set foot on a small farm in a developing country. If they knew and worked with smallholder farmers, they would understand that switching to hybrids that require new seeds to be purchased each season represents a complete break with a centuries-old tradition of seed saving, not to mention the added cost of purchasing fertilizer and pesticides. Moreover, hybrids often require more water, adding to the burden in most rural farming areas.

Industrial and smallholder farming represent polar opposites on the agricultural spectrum. Industrial farming has had every imaginable kind of support over the years but, as the global food crisis in 2008 clearly demonstrated, it has serious handicaps that make it both vulnerable and unable to adapt in periods of emergency. At that time, the price of imported food had dramatically increased in many poor countries. With no significant domestic food production to cushion the blow, the result was widespread social and political unrest. Closer examination of the underlying causes of the "Arab Spring" of 2011 make it clear that in places like Egypt and Yemen, the spike in food prices was a significant contributing factor to those popular uprisings. Rather than seeing industrial and smallholder farming as enemies, why not change the game and view smallholder farmers as an under-utilized asset—thinking small could be the next big thing in agriculture. Smallholder farmers could become the principle agent for a worldwide experiment in developing sustainable and ecologically sound farming practices that would compliment agribusiness, and at the same time serve as a domestic buffer against spikes in imported food staples. What better place to begin the experiment than in Haiti? Gustave and Rosemary have already started.

Community building

The new spirit of community among the farmers in our program warrants a closer look.

Small-scale farmers in Haiti, as in many other parts of the world, live from crop to crop. For the most part, they do not have bank accounts or cash reserves. One misstep that leads to a lost crop, and that family is at risk. There is much good will among the farmers, who do help each other out, particularly at harvest time. But there is still an innate caution that holds them back from new forms of collaboration. That is where our cooperative model enters the picture. As we built up trust, the participating farmers felt more comfortable contributing seed to a common bank, for example. The farmers' committee was something completely new, but it soon earned the respect and support of the entire community. Of course, the most tangible benefit of this new method of collaboration was increased income for the participating farmers.

The success of the overall agroforestry cooperative model is due to its ownership by the farmers themselves, and the leaders from among them who make up the farmers' committee. And at the heart of that committee is a new form of open consultation when dealing with issues affecting the farmers. And not only farming issues, but any issue affecting the community can be discussed. All financial transactions are in the open. Every member must treat the others with respect or face censure by the group. When inevitable disputes arise, the members must first reach a consensus on the best method for resolving the matter. Another interesting procedure, previously unknown to me, takes place when there are new people in a meeting: everyone present will be asked to introduce the person next to them, rather than introducing themselves—a great way to get to know your colleagues.

I have sat in on some two dozen of these farmers' committee meetings over the last two and a half years, and never once been asked for money. I mention this because there is a prevalent misconception, particularly among NGOs, that poor and illiterate Haitians cannot be trusted to run programs. My experience is very different, having watched this committee deal effectively with a wide range of issues over the years. But it was cholera that provided the most poignant proof.

When cholera struck Haiti in late 2010, there was widespread panic among the population because they had no idea how to deal with the disease. People were dying agonizing deaths in front of their families, in what seemed like only hours after contracting cholera. As the first few deaths occurred within the extended farming community in which our program is based, the entire population turned to the farmers' committee for leadership. No one from any level of government—or any NGOs for that matter—had come to the area to talk about the outbreak. The farmers were entirely on their own.

I happened to be attending the farmers' committee meeting when this issue was initially raised, and their first request was not what you might expect. The farmers asked if there was a way for them to be trained so that they could help prevent cholera in the area. Within a few days, fifteen of the farmers and nursery technicians had been given a short training by Partners in Health, the exceptionally effective NGO which, along with Doctors Without Borders, had taken the lead in responding to the outbreak throughout the country.

Within a week of the meeting at which cholera prevention was discussed, I returned with a truckload of soap. Most farm households do not have a toilet, and consequently they do not wash their hands after a visit to the bushes. I realized it was not enough just to drop off the soap, so we called the community together at the main nursery. With a few hundred people watching, I conducted a demonstration of how to wash your hands. We had a basin of water on a small table, and several children helping with the demonstration. I turned it into a game of counting the number of times we scrubbed our hands and washed up past our wrists. I was struck by a vivid memory of my mother teaching me the same thing as a child, along with her admonition to always wash up past your wrist.

All the nurseries in our program became involved in cholera prevention, running regular sessions for anyone from the community to come and learn the basics of prevention, how to identify the symptoms, and what to do if you contracted the disease. We brought in thousands of bars of soap and liquid hand sanitizer, and these were distributed from the various nurseries.

One afternoon, Wilson Noel, a technician in the main nursery, received a call on his cell phone from someone who had just come across a boy who lay dying on a road close to the nearby farming community of Morancy. Wilson jumped on a motorcycle and within a half hour was back at the main nursery in Mapou with a barely conscious fifteen-year-old boy named Florvil. When he had become violently ill with cholera, Florvil's family had not known what to do: they were concerned that the whole family would die if they had any further contact with their son and so, having nowhere to turn to for help, they abandoned the boy on a road to die. One can only imagine what an agonizing decision that must have been for the parents. No one approached Florvil as he lay on the road out of the same fear and lack of knowledge that guided his family; luckily, one bystander knew to call the cooperative. Once at the nursery, the farmers gave him the basic oral rehydration mixture they had learned about from Partners in Health, made with specific proportions of salt, sugar and water. This stabilized him and Wilson then took him by motorcycle to a hospital in Gonaïves. Within a week Florvil was completely restored to health, back with his family, and attending school as usual.

For Haiti to undergo any real and lasting transformation as a nation, a new sense of community must be built from the ground up. Our program is making a contribution to this process by training farmers in a fair and transparent collective decision-making process, which is also nurturing natural local leadership. It started off as a way to manage an agroforestry cooperative, but has already evolved into at least one component of a new model for rural self-governance.

Sustainable business model

Few words are so widely used, but so misunderstood, as the term "sustainable." It is bandied about everywhere with such abandon that it has lost all meaning.

There are two applications of the word that pertain to my work in Haiti. The first is sustainable agriculture, which I define as growing food in a manner that does no harm to either the environment or biodiversity, and which contributes to a healthy rural economy.

The second application of sustainable is in connection with NGO programs in general. Too often, in reality, the word is interchangeable with "aid dependency." I believe that a specific project or program in a developing country can be deemed sustainable if it meets the following test: is it still operating effectively three years after the original NGO has stopped providing core funding and has ceased to oversee the day-to-day operations of the program? This applies not only to NGOs, but also to programs that receive funding and/or oversight provided by donor governments, the United Nations, or other international institutions.

A small confession: as smug as the above sustainability test may sound, most of the past projects I have been involved in did not meet this criteria. I am in debt to Timberland, and more specifically to Jeff Swartz, for making me take a hard look at the true meaning of sustainability. His emphasis on striving for the maximum social impact with the strategic use of minimal financial resources forced me out of the comfortable NGO zone of thinking that, simply because you are doing work to better humanity, the universe should supply an unlimited amount of funding. I can hear NGOs objecting en masse, although many know that this is true. And I am the first to acknowledge that, in striving to deal with immediate needs in a country like Haiti, it is not easy to incorporate an exit strategy that ensures your project will continue and thrive without you.

The first thing I had to do was to frame our agroforestry program differently in my mind. The traditional method would have been to think about the desired impact and work back from there to figure out what it would take to achieve this specific result, translate that into a budget, raise the money, and implement the program. But I now had a chance to step back and start with a clean slate. I realized that our program would work better if we viewed it as a business model, albeit a non-profit version. Go into a given community of farmers with a model that combines growing trees and improving food crop output, train them from day one to own and operate the project, build in several diverse income streams, and then plan to walk away after three years and have it be self-financing and self-managed without direct involvement of the NGO. Thinking of the program in this way meant that it was designed to transform a group of farmers rather than simply direct them. Our goal was to create a farmer-owned agroforestry cooperative model that could be implemented anywhere in the country, with each cooperative—an economic unit defined as people jointly operating an enterprise and sharing equally in its benefits—becoming independent and self-financing after three years. As was mentioned earlier, the participating farmers in the pilot program are now in the process of becoming their own legal cooperative, Alyans Ti Plantè-Gonaïves.

Stepping out of my NGO comfort zone, I have been actively working with Timote over the past two years to create non-profit business elements within the framework of the cooperative. We had already envisioned that participating farmers would volunteer to grow trees as payment for an agricultural service to improve food crop yields and bring them higher income. But the bigger question was how the overall program would operate without external funding. This led us to create a menu of seven options for every cooperative to utilize, depending on what the farmers feel will work in their area, itemized in the following list. Each option has been conceived as one business element that can generate income for the cooperative to allow it to cover the cost of ongoing operations once we stop providing funds after three years:

- **Selling trees**—Each cooperative is designed to generate an average of one million trees a year. While most are for the farmers' own use, there are enough to be able to sell a portion. After two and a half years of operation, the first cooperative in Gonaïves will begin offering 100,000 trees for sale in November, 2012. Based on what we learned from this experience, the plan is to make this a permanent feature of all future operations.
- **Seed bank surplus**—The farmers in the Gonaïves pilot have, until recently, given back the same amount of food crop seeds as they received at the start of the growing season. We have begun to experiment with increasing the return policy to 15 percent above what they received so that we begin to build up a surplus that can either be sold by the community as seed to farmers in the area who are not part of the program or, if the quality is not high enough, sold in the market as grain. Either way, the income goes to the cooperative.
- **Marketing and sales**—Still a work in progress, the idea is to sell the farmers' output in bulk in order to fetch a decent price—saving them the task of having to sell it themselves in local markets or sell their crops to an agent at a lower price. When they sell to an agent,

that individual resells the food and pockets the difference. Eventually the farmers can start planning their crops based on advance agreements to purchase specific items. The plan, by the end of 2012, is to be marketing a good portion of the output of our farmers, with a small overhead on the sales going to the cooperative.

- *Microfinance*—With a one-time investment of capital, combined with the cost of training two people to manage the operation, we plan to have a microfinance component in place by September, 2012. Loans of between 2,000 and 30,000 Haitian gourdes (roughly from US$50 to US$750) will be given for repayment in one to six months. Loans will be limited to groups of five or six women who form a lending circle, with the group assuming responsibility for ensuring repayment. The money will be used by the women to finance purchases for their farms, as well as equipment that will allow them to turn their crops into saleable products. We estimate that within four months from the start of operation, this microfinance service will become a modest profit generator for the cooperative.

- *Farmer field schools*—We currently provide ongoing training for the participating farmers. But our plan is to launch a 90-day intensive training course, in segments over the course of a year that correspond to down times in the agricultural cycle. Farmers will earn a certificate and, in addition to learning basic farming techniques, they will get instruction in basic financial literacy and other life skills. Farmers already in the cooperative will pay a modest amount for the school course, but we will be approaching donors to underwrite scholarships for other farmers in the area. Our hope is to make this a permanent program element, with profits going directly to the cooperative.

- *Tree seed gathering*—Training has begun in the art of tree seed gathering. This is not just a matter of finding trees and picking off the seeds, but of identifying "mother trees" and harvesting the seeds at a precise time. By gathering our own seeds for our tree nurseries, we are able both to save more on the seeds used for planting and to generate further income by selling the surplus.

- *Land reclamation*—The most ambitious idea for generating income, as yet untested, is to have the cooperative paid to reclaim degraded land and turn it into productive farms using agroforestry techniques. This plan needs more work before it can be implemented. However, the farmers of Haiti would seem to represent the best resource to take on restoration of the denuded landscape. And the most likely recipe for success is to use trees to turn that land into productive farms that generate income. When trees have an immediate economic value, there is a reason for protecting them from the dual ravaging forces of charcoal gatherers and wandering livestock.

As each cooperative within the program becomes independent and self-financing after three years, they become part of a network of cooperatives with a financial link to the parent organization, drawing once again on the Timberland play book. The Smallholder Farmers Alliance will sell them tree and crop seeds, although each cooperative will always be free to find the best deal if we are not competitive. We will help the various cooperatives to work together to market their trees and food crops, leading to savings of scale. We will also cover the salaries of three agronomists for each cooperative on an ongoing basis, ensuring that there is good technical input and as a way to monitor that the cooperatives continue to function effectively and meet a strict code of conduct. In addition to full transparency and the following of democratic principles, central to that code of conduct is keeping out of politics. We are keenly aware that with the success of the program comes the temptation for it to become politicized, particularly as it is based on blocks of 2,000 well organized farmers managing each cooperative.

In 2013 we plan to have completed the basic guidelines for replicating the Smallholder Farmers Alliance model. The plan is to create as many cooperatives as we can throughout the country. But we will also be making the details available as open-source development technology. While they will need to come up with their own name and secure their own funding, anyone will be able to take the model and implement it. We will provide some technical assistance if requested, but our hope is that this agroforestry model will start popping up around the country.

Two-part harmony

The experience of working with smallholder farmers in Haiti has taken shape as a vision in two parts.

First, that an agroforestry revolution spreads throughout the country as a grassroots movement far beyond the scope of any one NGO. In the process, I think we can show the potential for smallholder farmers to go from being marginalized to leading the way in sustainable food production. We began in 2010 in Gonaïves, and will soon have more cooperatives established in other parts of the country. Hopefully, within a few years, we will have created a network of cooperatives, as other organizations begin applying the open-source technology that we will soon be making available.

The second part of the vision has to do with the "Haiti experiment": the proposal outlined in Chapter 5 for Haiti to become the site for a 10-year, country-wide research study in how to significantly improve the use of development aid. Agriculture is one vital component of this larger research, and I am suggesting that the smallholder farmers in Haiti could engage in this experiment on behalf of smallholder farmers the world over. According to census data from the UN Food and Agriculture Organization (FAO), there are around 525 million farms in the world. Together they provide a livelihood for about 40 percent of the global population. Nearly 90 percent of these are small farms, defined as having less than two hectares of land, and occupying roughly 60 percent of arable land worldwide. Humanity faces a massive global food crisis unless production rises significantly in the next decades, and smallholder farmers are central to meeting that challenge. They need to be enlisted, and their counterparts in Haiti are a great place to start.

5

TURNING THE TABLES:

Haiti as a Model for the World

HAITI, 2012. Haiti is part of the Western hemisphere by geography, and the Caribbean by culture and tradition. But in reality, it exists in a world apart from both. After slaves rose up en masse and defeated Napoleon's army, the major powers of the day, in an effort to limit the contamination of slave revolt, mounted a long and coordinated campaign to isolate the new nation. Other countries in the region suffered under colonial occupation, but only Haiti was brought to the verge of bankruptcy by having to buy back its own citizens from France. Many nations in this part of the world have endured foreign intervention, but after nineteen years of US occupation (1915 to 1934), Haiti was left without local, regional, or national capacity to govern, while burdened until 1949 with paying the interest on loans taken out to make slave payments to France. While other countries in the hemisphere have faced the indignity of domestic dictatorships that were bankrolled from abroad, only Haiti was left with an economy that is still largely based on foreign aid.

But, as explained in Chapter 1 about the history of Haiti, foreign intervention is only half the story. Those forces alone would not have been sufficient to deliver Haiti to its current state, had they not been aided and abetted by the deep divide between the minority mixed race elite and the majority poor black population. This great social divide has plagued the country from its inception on January 1, 1804 to the present day, factoring in every step of Haiti's tortured history.

The combined external and internal forces that have beset Haiti for more than 200 years have also made it more vulnerable to natural disasters, such as hurricanes and earthquakes, and ensured that the inadvertent introduction of cholera would become an epidemic rather than an outbreak.

There are few nations on earth that, while technically democracies, are so completely run by outsiders. The country's economy and the delivery of most of its basic services are in the hands of a shadow government. The money to run the country comes mostly from foreign donor governments that decide how it will be spent. These governments, in turn, give the money—supplemented by public donations during periods of crisis—to foreign NGOs for social services, to foreign private contractors working on infrastructure projects, to the United Nations to provide security through the deployment of peacekeeping troops, and to the UN's World Food Programme to supply 6 percent of the country's food.

Haiti is a failed state. This is the technical term when a country's government is so weak or ineffective that it has little real control over its own territory. Breaking it down further, a failed state means that a government is unable to provide public services, has little management of its economy, is plagued by widespread corruption, patronage, and inefficiency, and is without the capacity to ensure public order. The litmus test of whether a state has failed is always at the community level. In poor areas throughout Haiti, residents turn to NGOs for health services, to the World Food Programme when there is a food shortage, to foreign contractors for jobs, and to UN peacekeepers when gunfire erupts. This, despite their distrust of foreigners and because this is simply the reality on the ground.

This litany of malaise is not the fault of any democratically elected governments in the past two decades, including the current one. Despite their best efforts, none of these governments has been able to overcome Haiti's unofficial "international receivership" status and the consensus within the international community that Haiti is beyond hope and that no amount of aid is going to do anything more than prevent the country from becoming the geopolitical equivalent of a black hole. Neither is Haiti's situation the fault of the individual NGOs that have valiantly, often in the face of tremendous hardship, managed to deliver public services that millions of people depend on. The problems, however, are all too real and the effect on the population all too devastating.

Follow the money

Lest the reader think that this is too dramatic and overstated, let me share with you a short analysis of the money coming into Haiti since the earthquake.

First, how much money are we talking about? To get a realistic picture, you need to look at how much money it takes to run the country and where that money comes from. The following figures cover the period from January, 2010 (when the earthquake occurred) to May, 2012—twenty-nine months in total, or one month short of two and a half years.

Public donations from foreign governments total roughly US$6 billion over those twenty-nine months. Note that this refers only to money *spent* and not what has been pledged, but is not yet disbursed. During this same period, private charitable donations to NGOs for work in Haiti totaled some US$3 billion.

Apart from the above-mentioned US$6 billion, foreign governments donated an additional US$1.9 billion to cover the cost of the UN's peacekeeping mission (known by its French acronym, MINUS-TAH), for the twenty-nine months. Governments also donated US$482 million to the World Food Programme (WFP) during this period, money that was used to purchase and distribute 6 percent of the food consumed in Haiti. MINUSTAH and WFP, respectively, provided these figures. In the interests of accuracy, US$118 million of the funding to WFP is deducted from the running total, because it is already counted as an emergency contribution in 2010 as part of the US$6 billion amount from governments.

In recent years, the operating budget of the government of Haiti has consistently depended on 60 to 70 percent from foreign aid and only 30 to 40 percent on revenue from taxes, loans, and other sources. Combined aid and revenue expenditures for the twenty-nine months came to approximately US$3.8 billion. But discounting the 60 percent aid portion—because it is counted within the US$6 billion from foreign governments—only the revenue portion gets added to the running total: US$1.54 billion.

In order to get a complete picture, I would estimate that the rest of the UN operation in Haiti (not including MINUSTAH and WFP) has involved the expenditure of around US$185 million. This is only a conservative estimate; the actual figures are all but impossible to gather. I am including the UN here, because the various agencies such as UNICEF, the UN Development Programme (UNDP) and others all contribute to the effective provision of public services in one way or another.

Adding it all up, the total cost of running Haiti for twenty-nine months is roughly US$13 billion. Of that, US$11.5 billion, or 88 percent, is foreign aid, both public and private. The government of Haiti had direct control over the disbursement of only slightly less than 30 percent of the money used to run the country, of which 60 percent came from foreign donors. Looking at it another way, the government of Haiti's direct revenue accounts for only 12 percent of what it costs to run the country.

There comes a point where common sense trumps any possible explanation or economic theory regarding a situation like that of Haiti. No sane person living in, or visiting the country, could state with confidence that US$13 billion—which translates to an average of close to US$15 million a day, seven days a week, over twenty-nine months—has made a significant contribution to improving the lives of the majority of ordinary Haitians. Yes, there has been some progress, even pockets of significant improvement, but nothing even remotely commensurate with this level of funding.

So where did the money go? The bulk of it went to five sources: foreign NGOs, foreign private contractors, two UN operations (MINUSTAH peacekeepers and the World Food Programme), and the US Department of Defense. Whether or not they represent services that would better be provided by a well-functioning government, the expenditures for MINUSTAH peacekeepers and the World Food Programme are transparent. The funding they receive corresponds directly to services provided. The same is the case for the Department of Defense being repaid for its impressive security operation, which included reopening and managing the airport in Port-au-Prince and helping to maintain security in the capital. More challenging is tracking the foreign aid channeled through NGOs and private contractors.

It is often said that only 15 to 25 percent of aid provided by foreign governments ever makes its way to those it is intending to benefit at the local level in any developing country, including Haiti. This is not a scientifically derived number, but a rule of thumb used by development professionals familiar with the field. And while it cannot be the sole basis for drawing conclusions, this informal percentage can be a starting point for looking at a problem very much at work in Haiti, but one that is endemic to the entire field of development aid.

To understand the process, you first have to realize that development aid is no longer a direct transfer of money from a rich country to a poor country. Regardless of the military, political, or security reasons one country gives money to another, and what the donor expects in return, the actual transfer of the money has become a process in and of itself. This is where NGOs and private contractors come in. Donor funding begins its journey from a rich country to a poor country by entering a complex "development money management system" that was originally intended as a way to ensure efficiency and accountability, but which has become as dysfunctional as subprime mortgages or the banks that backed them. The money that enters the system is not managed efficiently, and ultimately does not equal the services provided on the ground in developing countries. A theoretical example is the best way to explain how it works.

Assume government "A" decides to give Haiti a grant of US$150 million. In this fictional scenario, the funds are intended to improve watershed management, in one agricultural region of the country, by working with 18,000 small-scale farmers over a three-year period. The money goes to government A's overseas aid department, in which the staff undertake a study to determine the needs on the ground because they are not able to use existing data—it's a rule somewhere. The study turns out to be a bit more expensive than planned, because they can only use research firms from country A (another rule); on top of that, the researchers end up having to subcontract much of the work when they get on site, because they are unfamiliar with the location. Armed with an expensive study, the overseas aid department next finds an NGO or private contractor to be the recipient of the grant; but that recipient must be from country A (a rule). So the first thing the NGO/contractor does is to extract an overhead amount at their headquarters operation in country A for oversight, management, accounting, and travel to Haiti. The Haiti office of that NGO/contractor then needs to scale up; so they take out some funds to add staff and cover overhead. But each staff person requires a vehicle, and these can only be purchased in country A and shipped to Haiti. No used vehicles are allowed (an insurance rule), which adds to the overall cost. Each vehicle will need to be driven by one dedicated driver per vehicle, and each vehicle needs to have a dedicated security person to be in the front passenger seat at all times: so more staff is hired. All of these expenditures need to be overseen by a Haitian accounting firm. The NGO/contractor does not, of course, actually implement the grant themselves. They hire consultants, preferably from country A, who help them find smaller NGOs, local Haitian organizations and various faith-based groups to serve as subcontractors. Each subcontractor must take out overhead and management costs, and they each require a vehicle that must be purchased in country A and shipped to Haiti. Each subcontractor must also have their own external accounting firm to work with the main NGO/contractor's accounting Haitian firm, which, in turn, works with the accounting firm in the headquarters of the NGO/contractor in country A working with government A's auditors. The subcontracted NGOs and local groups in Haiti do not actually do the work, of course. They, in turn, subcontract to the associations that all small-scale farmers in Haiti are members of. Each association quite reasonably takes out a percentage for overhead and administration, and what is left of government A's grant is finally disbursed to the farmers to do the work. If each layer in the filtering system takes out between 7 and 10 percent, you begin to see where the money goes.

The 18,000 farmers doing the actual work of watershed management in this fictional account will be engaged in planting trees, terracing slopes, digging irrigation ditches, stabilizing river beds, and other related activities. Let's say they work full time for two and a half out of the three years of the grant period. Based on the premise that 25 percent of the grant reaches the final beneficiaries, this translates to US$3.20 a day for full-time work. Over the course of two and a half years, each participating farmer will receive US$2,083 out of US$150 million.

This raises a question: why would politicians in country A not be horrified when reviewing the final report of how taxpayer money was used? The answer is that the money is justified by statistics in official reports. As long as those statistics look good, everyone on the donor side is happy. As you might expect, every step in the development money-management system is designed to generate statistics. This adds more costs at every step. More importantly, it greatly affects the final operation on the ground, since every action must translate to an inflated statistic that justifies the funding, even if it means that the program being funded is not as effective as it could be.

But if the generation of statistics is built in to such a degree, why does this not result in a complete picture? In the final report, the statistic about each farmer getting paid US$3.20 a day would be almost impossible to find. Instead you would see that support was provided to 18,000 farmers who had an average family size of 5.7 (official UN statistic for Haiti) and so the "impact" of their income would accurately be recorded as having benefited 102,600 people and not 18,000. The participating farmers all live in communities where a further 200,000 people received secondary benefits through increased local commerce, and that is further recorded as part of the overall impact. The tree seeds that the farmers planted would be recorded as if they all grew into mature trees, even though most would never germinate because of a decision that it was too expensive to grow the seeds in tree nurseries. The terracing of slopes will get translated into the impact of each terrace on the total acreage of the farm on which it was created, even though only 20 feet of the terrace might cross one end of a farmer's field. The irrigation ditches will be measured by the impact on all the fields served by the larger irrigation system, even though the ditches built by the program correspond to only a fraction of the existing system that was built entirely by others. And so on. Translating programs into happy statistics has become an entire industry.

Each layer in the development money-management system extracts a percentage along the way. But the story does not end there. It is necessary to factor in the impact of duplication and disappearance in reducing the overall impact of development aid. Many of the programs being funded overlap with other similar programs. But in Haiti, as in other countries, there is almost no coordination between the various governments that provide money; hence, the duplication. Another norm in foreign government funding is that most of the programs are only designed to last as long as the funding flows. Once the funding stops, the program disappears along with any trace that it ever existed. Failure to build the capacity of the implementing NGOs, or the corresponding Haitian government ministries, means that once development aid stops for a given program, there is no one left who knows how to manage the operation or generate the revenue needed to continue.

As it stands now, there are only two points at which government donor funding is monitored: before it enters the development money-management system and when it "emerges" in the form of performance statistics. Along the way, the various NGOs and private contractors are not required to tell the government of Haiti what they are doing, or to be transparent about how the money is being used: they answer only to the government providing the funds.

This is not intended to be an indictment of a vast network of co-conspirators, but a simple story of how a system that was created in the 20th century with the best of intentions has gone wildly out of control in the 21st. Everyone thought it would be self-correcting by virtue of the number of checks and balances that were built in. There is no conspiracy to be routed out, but rather incremental steps by large numbers of people in many countries, collectively and over time, that have created an incredibly complex system that is entirely without the capacity to adapt in a meaningful way. Change will come about only by intervention. And now is the time for that intervention.

The Haiti experiment

When plots got particularly tangled towards the end of Greek tragedies, writers such as Euripides often employed a literary device known in Latin as *deus ex machina*. An actor playing a god or goddess would be lowered by a crane and, while suspended above the stage, would momentarily stop the action to explain how a seemingly fatal plot twist gets resolved: a new character is added, or an event revealed, that has not been foreshadowed thus far in the drama; or sometimes characters previously killed would be brought back to life because they are key to the next scene. While there is no easy resolution to the tragedy unfolding in Haiti, there may be a case for employing the diplomatic and development equivalent of the *deus ex machina*.

President John F. Kennedy expressed it best in a remarkably prescient speech in 1961 in which he said,

> Although our aid programs have helped to avoid economic chaos and collapse, and assisted many nations to maintain their independence and freedom—nevertheless, it is a fact that many of the

nations we are helping are not much nearer sustained economic growth than they were when our aid operation began. Money spent to meet crisis situations or short-term political objectives while helping to maintain national integrity and independence has rarely moved the recipient nation toward greater economic stability.

Taking up the spirit of those words, I would like to propose a ten-year experiment that uses the country of Haiti to explore a new model of development assistance, which, if successful, could benefit the world. In the same way that the European Recovery Program, or the Marshall Plan, helped to rebuild the economies of that region following World War II, Haiti could be helped to rebuild itself by pioneering an entirely new methodology that replaces the current broken system of foreign aid.

My goal is to begin a conversation, not to prescribe every step in the handbook for Haiti's recovery. This is a small country with a relatively small population. Virtually every index of human well-being is at, or close to, the lowest register on the scale. It is easy to get to. What better place to try an experiment for a new approach to development. And in order to get the discussion going, I am putting forward seven steps that I feel could guide the intervention in seven sectors: here is the 7x7 plan for the Haiti experiment.

Seven steps of intervention

The following are not meant to be sequential, and in varying degrees would need to be employed simultaneously in order to be effective.

1. *National consultation*

The future of Haiti must be determined by Haitians. And this means Haitians of all walks of life, not only politicians and those who are comfortable in front of a microphone. People throughout the country need to be heard in order to reach a consensus on the direction to be taken. There is at least one possible model for this process. Many countries in the Commonwealth create ad-hoc formal public inquiries in which distinguished non-political figures hold meetings where ordinary people voice their opinions on a specific, and often controversial, subject of national import. Called "Royal Commissions," this process can often take a year or more, until meetings have been held in as many cities, towns and hamlets as possible. Once appointed, the members of the Commission may not be influenced or removed by any authority. After canvassing the nation, their final report is not binding, but carries great weight because it represents the direct input of a broad cross-section of the population. As I have experienced several times, by the time a Royal Commission in Canada has concluded, it has often been responsible for building a national consensus around a given issue that imbues the final report with the imprimatur of holy writ.

2. *10-year development plan*

There is currently no long-term development strategy for Haiti. There are various plans for specific sectors, but certainly nothing that can be called comprehensive. This new national plan for recovery and reconstruction should cover a ten-year period and should be created by Haitians who have unfettered and unfiltered access to the best and brightest from around the world with experience in this area. Built into this plan should be a permanent mechanism for updating, reviewing and adjusting the plan as it moves forward. Nothing is potentially more dangerous than a brilliant plan that can never be adjusted in response to changing circumstances.

3. *Government-centered development*

There should only be one government in Haiti, and it should be the one that has been democratically elected. The programs and funding from foreign donor governments, along with NGOs, private contractors, the United Nations, its peacekeeping operation and its various programs, including the World Food Programme, should all be overseen and directed by the Haitian government.

This does not mean pooling funding or combining staff, but rather that the government is able to coordinate, prioritize, and integrate the various programs and services. Yes, there will be challenges. Checks and balances will need to be built in, and special attention given to preventing corruption. But the process of integration needs to start somewhere, and it will never happen by a simple show of hands by those willing to take the first step. It will take a groundswell of public opinion to get donor governments to agree; but this could be intervention at its finest.

4. *Performance-driven government funding*

As the Haitian government gains capacity and shows responsibility in managing its affairs, it should be rewarded with greater control of funding from overseas donors. But to get the ball rolling, there should be a flat 5 percent tax levied on all foreign government and NGO development money coming into Haiti. This money will be used to cover basic operations of the government, whose expenditures will be monitored by an oversight body that includes representation from the donor governments and NGOs. The tax should be phased out once specific performance milestones have been met by the government. At that point, the government should receive increased amounts of donor money to manage. There are lessons to be learned from the changes that have been made over the last few years in the management and coordination of external aid in Rwanda, in which the UN has played a key role. It is not a perfect model, but it warrants careful study.

5. *Government service training*

The government of Haiti is not going to improve in a vacuum. There needs to be a major initiative to train people in the field of public service. This can include both sending individuals abroad and bringing experts to Haiti, possibly leading to the establishment of a university program in this field. There should also be a call for young members of the Haitian diaspora to consider public service in their homeland.

6. *Financial transparency and accountability*

There are several good models to choose from, but the bottom line is that all those involved in implementing development, rebuilding, and reconstruction programs—the Haitian government, domestic and foreign NGOs and private contractors, the UN and its agencies—need to publically disclose all expenditures based on a standardized format. This information should be released in a timely manner and on a regular basis, with severe penalties or sanctions for failure to do so. The information should be compiled on a public website.

7. *Real time evaluation and monitoring*

There will surely be successes and failures, things that work well but could be improved, and situations where a near disaster yields a surprising insight. Throughout all sectors and all initiatives related to the 7x7 plan there must be an interconnected mechanism for monitoring and evaluating all major activities, but done in such a way that it does not get in the way of those activities. Built into this process should be a way to extract the lessons to be learned from this new approach to development funding that can eventually be transferred to other countries.

There will be a collective intake of breath by bureaucrats of all stripes upon reading these seven steps. That intake will be sufficient, if harnessed as wind power, to fuel a small nation for some considerable time. Each bureaucrat will have detailed, even compelling, reasons for keeping everything just as it is. But what better time to act than now and what better place to experiment than a small country like Haiti?

There is one more incentive to put on the table: saving money. I would like to suggest that development aid flowing from donor governments to Haiti could be reduced by one third and, if something like the 7x7 plan were implemented, it would still have a significantly greater impact than at previous levels.

Seven sectors to focus on

If this experiment is to work, the government of Haiti must have a direct say in the development policies that affect the daily lives of its citizens. This translates to seven key sectors that, together, can represent the foundation on which to rebuild the nation.

1. *Human rights*

   While the 7x7 plan is geared to improving the lot of all Haitians over time, none should be harmed while the country passes through what will be a disruptive period. Change is never easy and progress has many enemies. The weak and vulnerable must be vigorously defended by an independent and non-political body with the authority to intervene in cases of human rights violations. At the same time, there are existing conditions, particularly the situation of violence against women in tent camps and children being sold into domestic slavery—known in Haiti as "restivics"—that demand immediate attention.

2. *Agroforestry and charcoal reduction*

   Agroforestry combines growing more food with restoring Haiti's lost tree cover. Both can be achieved by enlisting the small-scale farmers who, while ignored for generations, still constitute the largest segment of Haiti's workforce. By helping these smallholder farmers to build on an organic tradition that uses non-hybrid seeds and no chemicals, we will be taking the first steps in creating a global agricultural insurance policy—a viable and productive alternative to the hybrid/GMO path that has already shown its dark side. Restoring tree cover only makes sense if it is balanced by reducing charcoal use. Introducing fuel efficient stoves and converting key industries off charcoal (distilleries, bakeries, and dry cleaners) would be a practical first step.

3. *Education and vocational training*

   Most Haitian schools are now private, requiring tuition beginning in Grade 1, and staffed by teachers with little or no training, or even a high school degree. Transforming this system must include a national program of teacher training, school and curriculum standards that are enforced, and the engagement of teachers, parents, and community groups to support education reforms. In the course of the change to state-funded primary schools, if not yet high schools, a transition period will be needed, during which at least some tuition is paid privately until the Haitian economy improves. And in the course of these changes, special emphasis should be given to the education of girls and basic literacy training for older women, both in response to research in many countries showing the long-term value to society of such an investment. Job training is another important factor, particularly when taking into account the kinds of jobs that will be required in the country's ten-year development plan.

4. *Health*

The work of Partners in Health represents a viable model for transforming public health in partnership with the government of Haiti. A particularly good example is the new teaching hospital that will soon open in the town of Mirebalais, thirty miles north of Port-au-Prince. Partners in Health has built this 180,000-square foot, 320-bed hospital to offer a level of care never before available at a public facility in Haiti. At the same time the hospital will offer high-quality education for the next generation of Haitian nurses, medical students, and resident physicians. This model should inform the design of a greatly expanded working partnership between NGOs and the Ministry of Health.

5. *Economy and employment*

While ensuring decent standards for workers, proper incentives must be built in to attract corporations to set up shop in Haiti. There are many pomising areas for economic development. Farming is now, and will continue to be, key to the economy, but small-holder farmers need the kind of basic assistance their counterparts receive in other countries. Tourism has enormous potential, and the country will have to work at changing its image in order for that to be realized. (Happily, the first steps in this direction have been taken this year by the Ministry of Tourism.) Manufacturing can be greatly increased if there is better infrastructure and a better climate for investment. The arts is a tremendous, untapped field, featuring everything from fashion to dance to video. A major public works push by the government would be an excellent way to finally rebuild Port-au-Prince and Jacmel, using Haitian firms instead of foreign contractors.

6. *Infrastructure*

One of the biggest improvements since the earthquake has been roads, and that should continue. The country needs an alternative to trees as its main source of power, which could include a combination of natural gas, hydro, and various green alternative technologies. Building codes that take into account earthquakes and hurricanes must be put in place and enforced. The lack of clean water and basic sanitation services must be a priority, to reduce the ongoing threat of cholera. Port facilities will have to be improved, particularly beyond the capital. Improving existing airports and building new ones is critical, especially outside of Port-au-Prince.

7. *Government services*

While some specific examples are covered in the above points, emphasis should be placed on the overall level of government services. Land title registration should be updated from the Napoleonic era, so that ownership is clear; the national police force—not an army—expanded, trained and properly funded; the justice system overhauled and corrupt judges rooted out; a comprehensive system of public transportation created. And the process of citizen access to government needs to be stripped of its colonial paternalism and made easy and, as quickly as possible, available online.

The current system for delivering foreign aid represents moral bankruptcy on a global scale. In Haiti, the problem has escalated to the point of creating a chronic dependence on aid that has usurped self-determination from the electorate. The country is drowning in badly-delivered foreign aid that floods locally as it makes its way relentlessly back to NGOs, government departments, contractors, consultants and vendors from the nations that provide it.

The dominance of industrial farming at the expense of smallholder farmers smacks of global materialism run amok, with Haiti as the worst-case scenario. The entire economy has been held back because of a dependence on imported food, coupled with the systematic withholding of support for the smallholder farmers who constitute two-thirds of the country's workforce.

I did not begin working in Haiti with the expectation of confronting either of these co-dependent phenomena. But I soon discovered that the country is a poster child for both. Ironically, it is the very scale of the resulting problems in Haiti, combined with its relatively small size, that makes it the perfect location for the 7x7 plan—a ten-year experiment to empower Haitians to rebuild their own country, while simultaneously exporting new approaches to delivering foreign aid and supporting smallholder farmers.

The time to act is now. If the moral imperative alone is not sufficient to warrant immediate action, then surely the coming food crisis is enough to tip the scale. It is unlikely that bookies will even take bets on whether there will be a food crisis in developing countries in 2013; the only viable wager will be on the scale of the disaster. The U.S. is in the midst of the worst drought in nearly half a century, while dry conditions have affected crops in parts of India, Russia, and South America. As news began to spread earlier this year of the projected weather toll on agricultural output, the price of various grains rose by as much as 60 percent over just four months. The situation is made worse by the diversion of around 40 percent of US-grown corn to produce ethanol, making the portion that is sold for food more expensive because of its scarcity. The price of US corn, which accounts for more than half the global market, has long been an accurate bellwether in predicting global food prices.

The ripple effect of significantly reduced output by industrial farms in 2012, along with low global stocks, will culminate in the first quarter of 2013 with yet another sharp increase in the price of imported food on the streets of Haiti and other developing countries that have been forced into a dependence on food imports. It is hard to imagine that this will not lead to a repeat of the 2008 global food crisis; but there is the very real possibly that it will be much worse this time around and potentially become a permanent, rather than episodic, feature of the global food situation.

The short-term response to the 2013 food crisis will involve rich countries handing out aid money so that those in poor countries will have cash to purchase expensive imported food. But the system is hopelessly broken and these actions, while necessary in the face of disaster, will not address the systemic nature of the problem. The sensible, sustainable and long-term answer lies in changing the way we deliver foreign aid, coupled with building a global food insurance policy through investing in smallholder farmers to increase local production and reduce dependence on industrial farm imports. I hope this book stimulates a conversation about these issues and contributes to building a grassroots constituency for change matched by bold action on the part of decisionmakers.

Final thoughts

Christopher Columbus landed on Hispaniola in 1492, coming ashore on the western end of the island that would later become Haiti. He was on a mission from Spain to look for gold. When his initial attempt failed, he came back the following year and spent several months exploring the interior, but once again failed to find gold. Ironically he was trekking through a mountainous area that had deep deposits of the precious metal, but it would be hundreds of years before geologists would detect it. Mining companies recently announced the discovery of what could potentially be one of the world's largest gold deposits:

an estimated 23 million ounces worth anywhere from US$20 to $40 billion. Christopher Columbus either walked over these deposits, or certainly within a few miles at most, taking into account where his base camp was set up and where the gold has been found.

The past two hundred years would certainly not warrant unfettered optimism regarding the potential of this discovery to catalyze meaningful change. I would suggest, however, that the true untapped wealth of Haiti is the potential of its people, released from the strictures that have held them back since 1804, to finally harness the spirit of their founding revolution and chart a new path... with a little help from their friends.

Bibliography

Alexander, Franz C. M. 1992. Experiences with African Swine Fever in Haiti. *Annals New York Academy of Sciences* 653:251–256.

Baldwin, Katherine and Nathan Childs. 2011. *2009/10 Rice Yearbook*. Washington, D.C.: Economic Research Service, US Department of Agriculture. January.

Bender, Thomas, Laurent Dubois and Richard Rabinowitz. 2011. *Revolution! The Atlantic World Reborn*. New York, NY: New-York Historical Society.

Birdsall, Nancy and William D. Save. 2010. *Cash on Delivery: A New Approach to Foreign Aid*. Washington, D.C.: Center for Global Development. 16 March.

Bourne, Joel K. 2009. The End of Plenty. *National Geographic*, p. 26.

Brown, Lester. 2011. *World on the Edge: How to Prevent Environmental and Economic Collapse*. New York, NY: W.W. Norton.

Bulletin of Science, Technology & Society 7:615–20.

Buss, Terry F. 2006. *Why Foreign Aid to Haiti Failed*. Washington, D.C.: National Academy of Public Administration. February.

Childs, Nathan (Coordinator). 1999. *Rice Situation and Outlook Yearbook*. Washington, D.C.: Market and Trade Economics Division, Economic Research Service, U.S. Department of Agriculture. November.

CNN. 2010. Larry King Live. 6 August.

Collier, Paul. 2009. *Haiti: From Natural Catastrophe to Economic Security. A Report for the Secretary-General of the United Nations*. Department of Economics. Oxford: Oxford University. January.

Alexander, Franz C. M. 1992. Experiences with African Swine Fever in Haiti. *Annals New York Academy of Sciences* 653:251–256.

Baldwin, Katherine and Nathan Childs. 2011. *2009/10 Rice Yearbook*. Washington, D.C.: Economic Research Service, US Department of Agriculture. January.

Bender, Thomas, Laurent Dubois and Richard Rabinowitz. 2011. *Revolution! The Atlantic World Reborn*. New York, NY: New-York Historical Society.

Birdsall, Nancy and William D. Save. 2010. *Cash on Delivery: A New Approach to Foreign Aid*. Washington, D.C.: Center for Global Development. 16 March.

Bourne, Joel K. 2009. The End of Plenty. *National Geographic*, p. 26.

Brown, Lester. 2011. *World on the Edge: How to Prevent Environmental and Economic Collapse*. New York, NY: W.W. Norton.

Bulletin of Science, Technology & Society 7:615–20.

Buss, Terry F. 2006. *Why Foreign Aid to Haiti Failed*. Washington, D.C.: National Academy of Public Administration. February.

Childs, Nathan (Coordinator). 1999. *Rice Situation and Outlook Yearbook*. Washington, D.C.: Market and Trade Economics Division, Economic Research Service, U.S. Department of Agriculture. November.

CNN. 2010. Larry King Live. 6 August.

Collier, Paul. 2009. *Haiti: From Natural Catastrophe to Economic Security. A Report for the Secretary-General of the United Nations*. Department of Economics. Oxford: Oxford University. January.

Crane, Keith, James Dobbins, Laurel E. Miller, Charles P. Ries, Christopher S. Chivvis, Marla C. Haims, Marco Overhaus, Heather Lee Schwartz, and Elizabeth Wilke. 2010. *Building a More Resilient Haitian State*. Santa Monica, CA: RAND Corporation.

Disasters Emergency Committee / Haiti Earthquake Facts and Figures. Available at: http://www.dec.org.uk/haiti-earthquake-facts-and-figures

Dubois, Laurent. 2012. *Haiti: The Aftershocks of History*. New York, NY: Metropolitan Books.

Échevin, Damien. 2011. *Vulnerability and Livelihoods Before and After the Haiti Earthquake*. Policy Research Working Paper 5850. Washington, D.C.: Latin America and the Caribbean Region, World Bank.

Farmer, Paul. 2011. *Haiti after the earthquake*. New York, NY: PublicAffairs.

Gluck, Caroline. 2012. *Haiti: The Slow Road to Reconstruction. Two Years After the Earthquake*. 12 January. Oxford: Oxfam.

Greenhill, Robert. 2011. *Private Sector Development in Haiti: Opportunities for Investment, Job Creation and Growth*. Geneva: World Economic Forum.

Headey, Derek and Shenggen Fan. 2010. *Reflections on the Global Food Crisis: How Did It Happen? How Has It Hurt? And How Can We Present the Next One?* Research Monograph No. 165. Washington, D.C.: International Food Policy Research Institute.

Hedlund, Kerren. 2010. *Strength in Numbers: A Review of NGO Coordination in the Field: Case Study. Haiti 2010*. Geneva: International Council of Voluntary Agencies (ICVA).

International Rescue Committee, American Red Cross, Haitian Red Cross, International Federation of the Red Cross, Save the Children, Mercy Corps, Oxfam GB, ACDI/VOCA. 2010. *The Market System for Rice in Haiti*. 7 February.

Kennedy, John F. 1961. *Special Message to the Congress on Foreign Aid*. Washington, D.C.: The Office of the President of the United States. 22 March.

Kristoff, Madeline and Liz Panarelli. 2010. *Haiti: A Republic of NGOs?* Washington, D.C.: United States Institute of Peace. 26 April.

Maguire, Robert. 2009. *Haiti after the Donors' Conference: A Way Forward*. Special Report No. 232. Washington, D.C.: United States Institute for Peace. September.

Murray, Gerald F. 1987. *Technology Without Literacy: Agrarian Innovation in Rural Haiti.*

New York Post. 2011. Questions Dog Wyclef's Haiti Fund. 27 November.

Office of the Special Envoy for Haiti. Available at: www.haitispecialenvoy.org

Oxfam. 2008. *Smart Development: Why US foreign aid demands major reform.* Boston, MA: Oxfam.

Ramachandran, Vijaya and Julie Walz. 2012. *Haiti: Where Has All the Money Gone?* Washington: Center for Global Development.

Roberts, Hugh (Editor). 2000. *Proceedings from the Soil, Food and People Conference: A Biointensive Model for the Next Century.* Willets, CA: Ecology Action.

Rice Situation and Outlook/RCS–2000. pp. 48–54. Washington, D.C.: Economic Research Service, US Department of Agriculture. November.

Schuyler, George W. 1980. *Hunger in a Land of Plenty.* Cambridge, MA: Schenkman Publishing Company, Inc.

Starke, Linda, ed. 2011. 2011 *State of the World: Innovations that Nourish the Planet.* New York, NY: W. W. Norton & Company, Inc.

The New York Times. 2010. Star's Candidacy in Haiti Puts Scrutiny on Charity. 16 August.

United Nations. Stabilization Mission in Haiti (MINUSTAH). Available at: http://www.un.org/en/peacekeeping/missions/minustah/facts.html

USAID Office for Food for Peace. 2010. *Best Market Analysis–Haiti.* Washington, D.C.: Fintrac Inc. August

World Food Program and FEWS/NET. *The Market System for Rice in Haiti 2010.* Emergency Market Mapping & Analysis Report. Port-au-Prince. February 7–17.

World Food Programme: Haiti. Available at: http://www.wfp.org/countries/haiti

Acknowledgements

The journey told through the pages of this book was not undertaken alone, and I want to thank those who walked with me. My wife, April, has been my rock throughout and my most ardent supporter. My mother, Mikky, helped keep me grounded in response to success, and optimistic in the face of challenge. Wyclef Jean and Jerry Duplessis were co-founders with me in creating Yéle Haiti and have been my guides, protectors, and champions throughout. Without them, this chapter of my life would never have been possible. Suzie Sylvain has been at my side for many years and her work was critical to Yéle's success.

The first steps of my Haitian journey began with a key introduction by Natabara Rollosson, followed by the creation of a consulting company with Roberto Ramos, Susan Jaramillo, and Andres Cortés (who also designed the book cover), whose support and creativity were invaluable from the outset. The early years of Yéle would never have materialized without the help of many colleagues both in the United States and Haiti, and I would particularly like to thank Maryse Pénette-Kedar, Richard Sassine, Gwynne Beatty, John Currelly, Nathalie Brunet, Henri Robert (Riro) Dominique, Sebastian Pétion, Miriam Padberg, Stephanie Armand, Bernard Fils-Aime, Seth Kanegis, Charmant Noncent, Jean (Jimmy O) Alexandre, Terrie-Ann DaCosta, Gabriel (Killer) Dorleus, Jean Deristil (Moise) Yonel, and Ismick Beljour.

The first five years of Yéle's work in Haiti were made possible with the financial support of Brad Horwitz through the Voilà cell phone company. Strategic support from Joey Adler and the ONEXONE Foundation was critical during our first year.

Tony Tempesta was a patient guide as we got Yéle's US accounting house in order, and David Hryck and David Mason were instrumental in steering us in the right direction as we upgraded our overall management.

Yéle's work following the 2010 earthquake involved hundreds of people, but I am especially indebted to Joe Mignon, Carlene Blanchfield, Claudinette Jean, Samuel Darguin, Lorena Gutierrez, Samuel Louis, Karen Pardini, Nathalie Philippe, Lexy Brooks, Darline Laguerre, and Marielle Moise for their critical roles.

I am very grateful for the leadership and dedication of Timote Georges, co-founder with me of the Smallholder Farmers Alliance (SFA), and to Jeff Swartz, Margaret Morey-Reuner, and Ethan Budiansky for the key role they each played in helping to develop this program. My thanks also to the newly formed board of SFA, in anticipation of the guidance they will be providing to Timote and me moving forward: Raymond Joseph (who also provided valuable edits to the book), Mark Newton, Rob Padberg (who has been a mentor to me), Eliette Pierre, Jean Ernst Saint Fleur, Jean-Frédéric Salès, and Jane Wynne.

The Clinton Global Initiative (CGI) has provided an invaluable service to Haiti by regularly convening leaders from all sectors involved in helping the country to rebuild, including government, and facilitating connections, collaborations and effective and measurable commitments to action. I am grateful to have been involved in CGI's Haiti initiative. President Bill Clinton deserves high marks for this and other avenues through which he is serving Haiti. Digicel Chairman and Founder Denis O'Brien also deserves mention for his role as a driving force in orchestrating CGI's Haiti focus.

Special thanks to Ward Johnston for reviewing all matters agricultural, Max Clermont for help with research, Deana Marie Howlett for her counsel, and Sharon and Blake Rowe for being patient listeners as updates on the book's progress dominated many a dinner conversation.

And a heartfelt thank you to Nancy Ackerman of AmadeaEditing, whose thoughtful and relentless editing has saved readers from many unnecessary diversions and many more lapses of good grammar, and Susan Lanzano for a careful fine-tuning of the final version.

About the Author

HUGH LOCKE was born in Canada in 1954. He began his professional career directing a nation-wide tree planting program for Katimavik, Canada's national youth service organization, and establishing a foundation and archives related to the work of forester Richard St. Barbe Baker (1889–1982). He went on to spend 20 years in the field of development, working with a wide range of governments, non-governmental organizations, corporations, and United Nations agencies on social, environmental, and economic programs which contributed to the common good. In 2005, he co-founded Yéle Haiti with musicians Wyclef Jean and Jerry Duplessis, and together they provided emergency relief, employment, education, and environmental services to the people of Haiti. Hugh stepped down as president in early 2011 to launch the Haitian-based Smallholder Farmers Alliance, of which he is co-founder and President. He currently advises and serves on the boards of a number of Haitian NGOs. He lives with his wife in New York state and commutes to Haiti.

Made in the USA
Lexington, KY
03 October 2012